FAMILY
RESEARCH (
AND HOW TO SOLVE THEM

Ian Waller

FAMILY
HISTORY
BOOKS

Published by
The Family History Partnership
the publishing imprint of the
Family History Federation
P.O. Box 62
Sherringham, Norfolk
NR26 9AR

ISBN: 978 1 906280 57 4

First published 2019

Printed by Henry Ling Limited
The Dorset Press
Dorchester DT1 1HD

CONTENTS

INTRODUCTION

Every family historians' nightmare is that an ancestor cannot be found or mysteriously vanishes. These brick walls, or more correctly "research challenges" can nearly always be overcome. You don't always have to demolish a brick wall, you can often go around it, climb over it or make a hole in it and crawl through. All will become clear as you read on. This is where you need to have or develop the characteristics of Sherlock Holmes or Agatha Christie and also be good at jigsaws.

The object of this book is to act as a guide to suggest to you the resources that are available to help resolve your challenges, why something may or may not work and why you should explore various possibilities to help demolish your brick wall. It will not explain to you where to find or how to use specific records. That information is readily available through archive catalogues, online material and the various record-specific guides.

When you have read the section make a note of the "Thumbs up" tip to help you focus on resolving your research challenge.

Searching for and locating records in which your ancestor may appear is sometimes not a simple process. You will need to know the circumstances for which the historical record was created to determine whether the record you think you can use can actually help. It will also indicate some of the reasons why you think it should help but doesn't. Yes, we can easily locate those ancestors who make it easy to be found, but we all have the elusive ancestor who seems to have made it a life-long pursuit not to be found or avoids officialdom. However, they can't avoid every record.

THE PROVERBIAL RESEARCH CHALLENGE (OR BRICK WALL)

If you have encountered a research challenge or even hit a "brick wall" then you have more than likely come up against the "unlucky thirteen". These, however, are not the only reason you will come across as you look for the missing ancestor. Situations like adoption, bigamy and even illegitimacy can prove even greater challenges. Be assured however, that every problem has a solution despite some challenges relating to poor research skills and knowledge. In most cases, through diligent research, solutions are inevitably available.

Research challenges will normally arise because of the "unlucky thirteen" fundamental errors or omissions:

1. Inadequate Research
2. You are undertaking narrow-minded research
3. You have researched the wrong individual or family
4. You have run out of ideas to try and trace an ancestor who has disappeared
5. You are searching in all the wrong places
6. They have changed their name
7. You are looking for the person YOU ARE looking for (think about it!)
8. You have different or conflicting "base" information
9. You are not using all the information that is available to you
10. You cannot read or have difficulty in interpreting the handwriting of the document.
11. You are not "power searching"
12. You haven't sought help
13. You are not being patient or persistent in your research and giving up too quickly.

The answer to many of the common challenges such as:

They have vanished off the face of the earth.

Not in the census – why?

There are two people with the same name born at the same time, in the same location, how do I know which one is mine when I cannot determine which family they belong to?

Can't find a marriage yet they were having children together.

The record which will give me the information has been lost or destroyed – what can I do?

Can't find a birth or baptism record.

They were born and did not die (believe me they are not immortal!)

can be found by following simple steps and adopting certain characteristics. You will need to be patient and persistent in your efforts; have a logical approach to your research; understand record limitations because none of the records available to us were created for family historians; know what sources to use; don't overlook the obvious, be single minded and make sure you have all the facts.

Initial searches online

There is no doubt about it that initially our task in tracing our ancestors is now slightly less complex because of the ever-increasing volume of records becoming available on the internet.

Today knowing how to get the best out of the databases (and indeed how to find them) is one of the most important initial skills that a family historian has to develop. However, be aware that few answers can be achieved using on line resources alone. Although you can search on a number of different sites and within different fields there is a tendency to fill out too many search fields which can be dangerous. "Less is more" because if one piece of information you entered does not match the information in the source document, you will not get a result and therefore may miss the person you are researching.

The following are a few preliminary and general tips to get the best out of online material and to help crack your challenge:

Don't be worried about how long your list of results is. It is better to trawl through a large number of results than to have missed the information because you have gone into too much detail in search fields, sometimes based upon other unreliable facts.

Remember it is often useful to do an exact search without a surname. Populating the forename field and one other important fact such as place or birth date/year will open up a wealth of detail to you to search. This is even more productive if you have an ancestor with a second and sometimes unusual forename. Surnames are very often wrongly interpreted or perhaps spelt in a different way to that which we recognise. Surnames are very often mis-transcribed because of difficulty in reading the capital letter at the start. In my own case the surname Burton had been mis-transcribed and indexed as Riwton. Would I have found it? – probably not without a fair amount of lateral thinking.

 Beware of the online transcription errors on surnames particularly the first letter.

When an illegitimate child takes the surname of the subsequent husband of the mother that can cause a challenge because you may not be aware of the husbands' surname. Many family historians do not consider that a mother of an illegitimate child could think of later marrying!

Family Reconstruction

It is very common to find that two people of the same name were born around the same time in the same town or village. One is your ancestor but which one?

The first and most obvious step is to try and kill off your ancestor. Always look for a death and burial because if you find that one has died then that goes a long way to resolving your challenge as only one lives to adulthood. If a child dies then very often the father's name is given in a burial register entry. (Not always, but if it does not, then you may still have a challenge in determining which one has died!)

There is an adage which states that once the impossible is eliminated then whatever remains must be the truth even if it is improbable. This can apply to family history research and may well be your clue to resolving your challenge. How do you move forward? You build up a theory then try to prove that the person you think is your ancestor isn't. If you cannot prove they are NOT your ancestor then they probably are.

 Kill off every ancestor before progressing to research further. That way you will trace the correct person.

Every family history challenge has two possibilities – you have too many choices that you cannot prove who your ancestor is or you have none. This is where you need to implement family reconstruction. Yes, it may be time consuming but in the grand scheme of things it will more than likely resolve your challenge. Your findings may also be rewarding in providing a connection you did not know existed or in providing more information about your family.

This is where you play detective and also build your jigsaw by building a timeline and life picture of the persons who you think could be your ancestor (see later). You will also need to research the extended families in order to confirm or eliminate. As you do so, patterns will emerge in such things as names, occupations and locations enabling you to piece together the facts which determine who your ancestor is.

This process is a very positive way of finding the right ancestor and in most cases proves successful, so the length of time it takes you is not wasted.

One aspect of family reconstruction which many family historians ignore is that of relatives raising children. By the process of reconstruction, it will also be possible to find the alternative to abandonment or adoption. Consider the possibility that the parents are raising a relative's child. Another possibility is when sisters "adopt" children who are related and typically the adopted children are in fact a brother and sister.

Family Reconstruction can also be aided by the use of DNA – more about how that can help overcome research challenges later.

MANY BRICK WALLS CAN BE DEMOLISHED
(SORRY FOR THE PUN!)

So, let us examine how we can overcome the challenges.

This can usually be achieved using six straightforward steps:

1. Review
2. Plan
3. Analyse
4. Extend your research
5. Interpret research correctly
6. Dig deeper

Your success in locating an ancestor or building a picture of your ancestors' life will be achieved only if there is a continuity of surname, that they appear in records, had consistent occupations and you can trace their mobility.

The most important stage in breaking through any challenge is the review. Irrespective of how confident you are that your research is complete, take a second look at your records and all other source information you have. You could easily have missed key information during your initial research. I would even suggest going back to a document if it has been some time since you last looked at it "just to check your information". You may well be able to pick up a vital clue that was not obvious to you or overlooked originally. As your experience grows you will realise that all information is valuable and be more aware of how a particular record can help.

Also consider what records have become available since your original research date. Some searching may be much easier if sets of records have subsequently been indexed or come online. As an example, it may be that a banns book has been deposited which was not available when you undertook your original research. Thus, you may find a clue to a parish at the time of the marriage which can lead to further evidence and additional research.

 Find out if any records have become available for research since you originally researched your ancestor. They may provide you with answers or at least clues.

In practical terms, and this won't work in every case, I suggest that you follow a similar path to that shown below.

Irrespective of your record keeping system, isolate and write down all of the information you have in a chronological way and decide on the extra information you need for the ancestor who has presented the challenge. By organising data chronologically, you may get ideas of where and in which type of record the vital information may be located.

Researching collateral lines could help. Was your ancestor staying with or visiting another member of the family in a different part of the country? Sometimes a woman may have given birth or baptised her child at her parents' home town or village some miles away from the family home.

Think about any other resources that may help you identify your ancestor. These will be discussed in greater detail later in the book.

Military and Naval service records could provide information not just about the soldier or sailor but also about wife, parents, siblings and children, particularly if they were born or baptised abroad while dad was serving in a foreign country. They will fall within the realms of the military chaplaincy. Many families accompanied serving military or naval personnel when the engagement to foreign climes was fairly long term. Some soldiers may have married and had children abroad as was often the case when serving in India or other parts of the Empire.

Wills are by far the best document to prove concrete relationships. These often give you additional family information, including details of the 'black sheep' or emigrant family members you knew nothing about or who might be the subject of your research challenge. You will also be surprised how many people actually left a will, so always check the appropriate jurisdiction even amongst the lower social classes.

Newspapers and specialist trade journals, as well as the staff magazines for employment organisations, are an undervalued resource. They can give family details, addresses, occupations, promotions, retirements, obituaries, as well as setting out achievements and perhaps showing character traits. Even small companies had staff magazines or newsletters. In my own research, loads of information was found out about an ancestor through a staff magazine of a small shoe factory in Northamptonshire.

Look at the original parish registers not just indexes or transcripts. The parish clerk or incumbent may have made some observations regarding your ancestor that the transcription does not show. An 1832 burial relating to one of my ancestors stated that the deceased had 'drowned in a dyke whilst drunk.' Baptism records of an illegitimate child will often suggest who the father is, perhaps recorded as a forthright comment, which will give rise to further research on that paternal line.

 Always review original records and don't rely on transcriptions except as finding aids.

Look for transcription errors or changes in how a name was spelt. Also, misinterpretation of gender is sometimes evident or has been assumed, where a forename could apply to either sex of a child. Francis and Frances are a common example.

Understand the record you are using. If you know why the record was created and its history you will understand it's pros and cons in helping with your research. Understanding a record can help you to see why your ancestor was or was not recorded in it.

Most family mysteries or dead ends are not true brick walls, all challenges have solutions as I have stated before.

Unlike the family history-based television programmes which rely on their entertainment value rather than educating us in processes, and where they present pristine certificates in brown envelopes to a researcher wearing white gloves behind the scenes of a record office, family history research cannot really be tackled in that way and certainly not in the timeframe those programmes imply. Family History research is a lifelong pursuit. It will never be complete because it will continue to grow as new resources become available, so don't give up on your research as the answer will still be out there.

COMMON MISCONCEPTIONS

Relations

Information provided by relations is not always accurate but usually contains an element of truth which can be investigated further. When you talk to relations the information you receive will inevitably be biased depending upon how well they related to or knew that person and whether they liked or disliked them. Don't let this cloud your own judgement. (When we begin research the first thing that is suggested is talk to your relations). Sometimes we don't have the opportunity to talk to granny or anyone that grew up with the person in question. Don't let that stop you. Throughout your research, and while you can keep talking to whichever relations you have around at the time, be it siblings, cousins, aunts, uncles etc. - you never know what information you can glean once you tell them what you have discovered. I have found the answers or several vital clues to various research challenges by doing this.

 Interview relations regularly as further gems can be forthcoming when they are prompted with information.

Whilst you may not want to develop an oral history you will be surprised how much information you can gather if you ask the right questions. Ideally you need to interview (and keep interviewing) senior members of your family by asking about the community they grew up in, their education and their friends and interests. The answers may lead you to vital clues for your research. Please don't interrogate as this inevitably closes doors. Most people will be interested in their own family, particularly if the person being interviewed had a close relationship with your ancestor.

History

It is easy, because we don't know any different, to judge historical events or society from a modern perspective. Once upon a time people took four days to travel between two places where today we can do it in a couple of hours! Think about, or better still, learn about life at the times your ancestor lived and then try to envision what the family's plight was or how society would have treated them. It has a bearing on the type of records you research. Think about the social standing of your ancestors and try and place them in their contemporary environment to better understand the records they may have appeared in or generated.

 Don't view historical events from a modern perspective. Things were very different even 50 years ago.

Find out how your family were affected by depressions, the world wars (and earlier wars), whether anyone was a member of, or associated with, groups that were discriminated against, what were the circumstances causing migration or even emigration. All of these will help you place your family in their contemporary environment and help you resolve the research challenge even if it does not give all the answers.

Mobility

This is one of the more challenging elements of research to resolve but there are many clues to help you do so. It is a complete fallacy that people did not move very far from their roots. I am sure we all realise that families and individuals could have moved across the world for many reasons.

Families migrated mostly for work and ultimately for a better life but few records might exist tracking such moves. Therefore, deductions need to be made from a variety of different records. Migration purely means a change in normal residence. Families moved both short and long distances mainly amongst rural dwellers leaving the land and moving into the major urban and industrial centres as a result of wage incentives or merely to find continuity of work.

The poor law administration played a great role in helping families move. Many of their agents were sent from industrial to rural areas to "recruit" so it is important in the first instance to establish whether this was a possibility and which agents went to a particular locality and when. This is particularly true at the time of the industrial revolution and throughout the 19th and early 20th centuries. Besides the records of the old and new poor law, criminal records may also be worth searching because people were sometimes incarcerated miles from home and on release from penal institutions settled in those areas principally because they were not known within the community. Some even changed their name!

Many people moved large distances particularly if they had a specific required skill and for basic economic reasons. Extended families often moved over a short period of time to the same locality if they followed kindred or associated occupations. That is a major reason to investigate collateral lines if you have been unable to trace a family. People who worked for organisations like the railways or Post Office could frequently move on promotion or transfer.

 If you have lost an ancestral family consider that they may have moved long distances for work or a better life. Review occupation and extended family groupings.

It is therefore important to consider that as a result of mobility, events such as marriage, birth of children and death may have happened outside the known area. They could have been in Scotland, Ireland, Isle of Man or the Channel Islands as well as perhaps further afield. Rule nothing out until you have eliminated. Many family historians don't look beyond England and Wales for their ancestors.

Emigration was usually undertaken with enthusiasm and the encouragement of other family and friends unless it was enforced by religious or political persecution. There were many schemes of assisted emigration which attracted families and sometimes just individuals. I have several individuals in my own family who upped sticks and went abroad on their own. Most assisted passage schemes meant the emigration would have been to the British Colonies, so government records would be the place to begin a search. There are many useful research guides available on the National Archives website relating to such moves.

Religious migration and emigration may also have been a factor in people moving long distances across the country, firstly to the major ports before boarding a ship and sailing across the oceans. Frequently such migration is well documented within the religious organisation's records and also within the destination country. This is no less true of religious immigration into the British Isles.

You may also find it useful to consider the practicalities of travel at the period of time you have your migration challenge. Before railways and reasonable roads, travel for the average individual or family would probably have been on foot or on horseback. The latter however, required a degree of wealth to actually own a horse. Travel by private coach would certainly have only been for the wealthy at a shilling a mile. The poorer members of the community may well have travelled using the local carter/carrier, suggesting that they may not have travelled far or done so in stages. Establishing the traditional routes of travel is the first priority in trying to locate a family's move.

Plotting migration patterns using a contemporary map will help considerably. It is unlikely that a family would have trekked over hills when they could follow public roads, canals or footpaths particularly if they had to carry their own belongings or pull a cart.

Some elements of travel need to be considered when working out how to locate a family that has moved:

Women generally did not travel as far as men. It is probably only newly married women who travelled with their husbands. Single women may have travelled significant distances away from their family home because they were servants travelling with their employers, so consider occupations and who they may have worked for.

Migration was generally along roads used by stagecoaches or other traffic. Many families frequently travelled no more than 10/15 miles from their roots or at the most from their village to the nearest market town. Contiguous parish searches should be undertaken as a matter of course when looking for lost ancestors if the clues about their whereabouts have dried up.

Coastal shipping also played an important role in migration. It was not unusual for someone from Tyneside, for example, to migrate on coastal ships to Norfolk or London and similarly using west coast shipping, which may well have included Scotland to Ireland and vice-versa. Finding a record of such voyages may however be problematic.

Try the Cluster Genealogy approach. Cluster genealogy is a research technique to learn more about an ancestor by examining a person's "cluster" which consists of the extended family, friends, neighbours, and even business associates and is an extension of family reconstruction.

From experience, it appears most migrants were unemployed (or had erratic employment), are adult and many were unmarried. Longer migrations were normally achieved over a series of shorter migration distances often with a period of residence in each locality. Most migrants appear to have come from rural communities as opposed to towns.

Death

I have often come across inadequate research where children who died in infancy or as youngsters later appear to have married and had large families! One of the biggest omissions leading to incorrect family structures is that we do not kill off each and every ancestor.

Another aspect of death is that gravestones were sometimes erected a long time after death and may not even be in the same cemetery or graveyard as an internment. Thus, the gravestone becomes a memorial rather than denoting a burial place. However, gravestones may contain vital clues like "alias" names but can, and do, contain inaccurate dates and ages. The information recorded on them is only as good as that provided by the informant.

Records

Although many of the records we rely upon for basic research are considered prime sources created under statute, they can only ever be as good as the information provided by the informant. Birth places in census returns are notoriously inaccurate for a variety of reasons. Ages at death can be way out because the informant is not a close relative, or someone aged 35 riddled with arthritis looked to be 60. It was not considered etiquette in some areas for a bride upon marriage to be shown as older than her husband so both are recorded as "full age" when in fact one is a minor. Often a given father's name is totally fictitious. I am suggesting that reliance upon one source or one set of documents is not recommended.

 Information on "official" documents is only as good as that provided by the informant. Many a time this is inaccurate so check more than one source for clarity.

Someone else's research:

Relying on research undertaken by someone else is, to say the least, foolhardy unless you check out for yourself its accuracy. It can however open the doors and may contain a gem so don't ignore it. Just exercise caution in using it in any other way than a "finding aid" until you have proved accuracy for yourselves. Many researchers are more than happy to share information and work in co-operation of expanding your common family history. One of the most frustrating aspects of using such information is often the lack of source details or blatant copying of information from one tree to another on the assumption that because its recorded it must be right!

 Don't rely on someone else's research until you have determined its accuracy.

Difficult periods:

Throughout history and for many different reasons research can prove difficult. Sometimes records have been systematically destroyed, others were never kept and some events happened that occurred before a record was made – or did they?

The 20th century is particularly challenging as many of the records have not been preserved. The Government introduced a policy of destroying records after a certain period had elapsed. Some census records have been destroyed or were not undertaken because of wars. Tax records are not available and many Coroners have destroyed their records along with other government departments after only 20-30 years, so this has left us with huge "gaps" in modern research. However, all is not lost as you will see later.

Between 1800 and 1837 many researchers come unstuck as this is the transition period between civil registration and parish records. Sometimes it means the difference between using online resources and having to get your hands dirty in an archive. If you don't have the knowledge to research it is a good idea to take a course or attend lectures etc. as today with online research you will very quickly arrive at this period. If you are unfamiliar with records or do not know what records to research then you may find it challenging to progress your family history.

Military research also has its challenges from World War One backwards. The majority of families would have members serving in the armed forces. I am sure most researchers know that around 40 % of army service records relating to the First World War period were destroyed by enemy bombing in World War Two. How many of you are aware however, that some of those records contained military service information as far back as the 1890s. (The most difficult period for army research is between 1890 and 1914 as no pay lists and musters of regiments exist for that period simply because the military authorities decided not to keep them anymore). This restricts information being available to those who, in the main, went to pension which is a relatively small proportion in comparison to the total number serving.

The Royal Navy however faired much better. From 1853 onwards continuous service records are generally available for whichever division your ancestor may have served in. One of the challenges is working out which division of the Navy an ancestor served in, particularly during the First Wold War. The main challenges of Naval research arise for the period before 1853. In most cases, unless your ancestor was an officer, you would need the name of a ship on which your ancestor served to access the ships musters and pay lists. This is the period when sailors signed up for "one voyage at a time" and often divided their service between Royal and Merchant ships. This can be problematic as few people will have an insight into which ship their ancestor served on pre-1853 unless family records so indicate.

Remember that post 1923 you need to apply to the appropriate record department for service records. Depending upon your closeness in relationship will depend on what information is released. There is also a statutory fee payable for this service which applies to all. One problem with the Royal Navy is that personnel serving in World War Two were given the option of taking their service record with them when they were demobbed. Such records may therefore be found in the family archive or may have been destroyed.

If you had an ancestor who was a Merchant Navy seaman then the period between 1857 and the end of World War One can be challenging as no official service records were kept. There may well however, be supplementary material such as Merchant shipping company records, crew lists and agreements, apprenticeships etc as alternative resources. A large number of crew lists from 1857 (when they were established) are held in Newfoundland and to find a record showing your ancestor you will need the official number of the merchant vessel.

 Ancestors who were at sea could have served part of their time in the Royal Navy and part in the Merchant Navy. If someone is referred to as a "sailor" they are probably in the Royal Navy and if a "mariner" the Merchant Navy.

Finding someone who emigrated or immigrated before the mid 1890s can also be problematic as few passenger lists exist for the UK prior to that time. It often means accessing the records held in both destination and originating countries. Luckily many are now available online to ease the burden. There is frequently more information about an immigrant than an emigrant so a search of the records in the destination country is inevitable.

Perhaps the most difficult period for research is that of the Commonwealth period 1649-1660 when Oliver Cromwell controlled the country and before the restoration of the monarchy. Cromwell outlawed the keeping of usual ecclesiastical records. Many people block baptised their children after record keeping was restored and some records have been compiled retrospectively. If your research takes you back that far then you are possibly already aware of some of the challenges.

A CLOSER LOOK AT BASIC RECORD INTERPRETATION AND UNDERSTANDING

I have already stated that information in records is only as good as that provided by an informant and this is very true. There are an inordinate number of errors which a family historian needs to be aware of even in the core records of civil registration, census, parish registers and wills.

Before you can even begin to resolve research challenges you need to be aware of record limitations so you do not pour over a record wondering why it does not give you the answer. I have already mentioned some very basic reasons in the preceding section but let us expand on those to give you a better understanding.

Civil Registration (Birth, Marriage and Death Post 1837)

There are so many challenges with the civil registration system that it is little wonder that family historians hit a difficulty when looking for an event as straightforward as a birth registration, record of a marriage or a death registration. Much of this can be attributed to human error and the fact we have the GRO indexes as a secondary source (compiled after the event).

Because we only have indexes to work from there is frequently an element of doubt as to whether we have identified the right person. That has become significantly easier because the GRO has now provided mothers' maiden names on their birth index entries and includes ages at death from the outset of the registration system in 1837. Many such ages can be notoriously inaccurate, and have earned the nickname of "Age Inflation"!

One of the most common challenges in breaking down a brick wall relates to our own inability to be broad minded when it comes to surnames in our family history, particularly as we are restricted to alphabetical indexes. This is quite often based on our own paradoxical ideas.

 Always be prepared to widen your research.

Missing from the GRO indexes

It is quite possible that registration events which took place have never been recorded in the GRO indexes. This is due to various reasons including inadequate returns from local registrars, particularly for marriages, or because of an error made by the record team at the GRO. The record team manually examined the registrars quarterly returns, then arranged the entries, transcribed the information and recorded the details on individual slips which were then sent for sorting and indexing by another team.

Imagine the number of times an error could be compounded! It does not mean that an event was never registered. Those seasoned researchers amongst us will remember that there were many handwritten entries added to the index books we used to look at before the digital age. Also, no one really knows how many register entries never made it to the national indexes. My own experience in researching indicates that it is always worth a try to "go local". I have had untold success in obtaining certificates from local registrars where no entry could be found using the GRO indexes. My guess is that this is because of omissions in returns being made to the GRO or through bad copying from those returns by the clerks who compiled the original indexes. This situation predominantly applies to births but can equally occur for both marriages and deaths.

Every local registrar has their own indexes and many are now digitised on ukbmd.org.uk where registrars have made those indexes available and from which you can apply to the local registrar for a certificate. (The cost is a little higher than a certified copy from the GRO and more expensive than a PDF copy). If the event is not recorded on the ukbmd databases then approach the local registrar anyway. My experience shows that most local registrars outside of London are co-operative and will send you a certified copy by return, usually handwritten. Some registrar offices maintain they are overworked and don't have time to search their records. Then a personal visit is needed. Beware however that local marriage indexes are usually by parish or chapel although some are consolidated by sub districts. You will usually be charged a statutory search fee on top of the certificate cost.

 If you are unable to find a record using the GRO indexes approach the local registration office. In many instances they will provide a certificate even when the index entry is missing.

One of the major obstacles in the marriage indexes is that of the marriage not being returned to the GRO because of the tardiness of vicars or authorised persons or only being indexed under one name. No matter how hard you look there is no reference to the "other party" where you can confirm you have found the exact entry.

One of the easiest ways to try and overcome this is by using www.freebmd. org.uk. If you find one party to the marriage and expand the page you can see the name of the other party. This confirms that you have found the correct marriage assuming you know the names of both parties. Otherwise you take a chance that you have identified the correct index entry, or try researching local parish marriage registers. If, however, the marriage took place in a register office you will not locate that information. Sometimes, if the index is only in one name and you don't know the name of the indexed party to the marriage, then you will need to undertake alternative research.

Generally speaking deaths are not usually as problematical but can suffer from the same indexing inadequacies.

Be aware also that when searching online many of the indexes are not configured in the same way as the GRO index so when recording of names changed to using only middle initials etc. or when more than two forenames are recorded the third initial will not always show and you may not find a match in your results field.

 If you cannot find a certificate reference on one site, check on all the commercial sites for index entries as each site have produced their own indexes and you may find an entry on one and not another.

The other thing to watch out for is late registrations of births and deaths. If a Coroner has been involved or if it took a while to discover the body, it was generally accepted that a death could not be registered until the body was located. Sometimes registration of death did not take place until the inquest was complete which can be some time after the date of death. Late registration of birth could happen when parents "forgot" to register. I have seen a late registration of a birth which occurred in 1881 not being registered until 1933! This, I think, is an exception but it does show that births were not always registered around the time of birth.

Birth anomalies

We normally calculate an ancestors birth year from information available in events later in life such as marriage or even death using information in other certificates, census or employment records. Most of the time people get their age basically correct but many genuinely did not really know how old they were, particularly those born in the earlier years of civil registration. Something as simple as this can cause a research challenge to the uninitiated. This is why we need to search indexes for a number of years either side of the possible birth year. You should also check all the documents you have for any inconsistencies in given ages.

Some births are registered much later than the event and, in any case, a six-week period for registration was allowed. Remember that birth registrations are recorded in the quarter that they are notified not the quarter in which the birth took place.

There is also the possibility that due to some muddle between parents, the same birth could be registered twice. This occurs where both the mother and father register the birth separately. They can be registered first in the registration district covering the place of birth and again in the registration district that one or other parent considers significant such as a home location. Don't rule this out – it happens. Often the only way to resolve this is to purchase both certificates and compare information. One or other may not contain the name of the father and just obtaining one could give the wrong impression of an illegitimate birth.

Illegitimacy can also be disguised by the fact that the child is registered against the mother's parents' names. Indeed, many grandparents did bring up their grandchild as their own. This child can also be registered before the marriage of the parents and may or may not include the father's name.

Sharing a birth certificate

It was not unusual for families to use the same birth certificate for more than one child where infant mortality exists. The birth registration for a child was often used for the birth of another same sex child. For example, if the first son was named John and he died as an infant or young child the next male birth would be given the same forename and so the original birth certificate was used. This can of course present a challenge or even a brick wall in later life because of age differences and also for differing birth dates. The second child who was given the same name and used the same birth certificate as the first may have celebrated his birthday as that shown on the certificate rather than the actual date of birth.

Until 1875 birth registration was also not compulsory and the onus for registration was on the Registrar and not the parents to comply with the registration requirements. Consequently, many early births escaped registration. It was considered by some families that if a child was baptised then there was no need to have a birth registered. Even after 1875 some births were not registered or were they? As previously indicated it is also wrong to assume that the birth was never registered so always check locally. Most children however, were baptised but be aware of the parents religious denomination for the record of such event.

Marriage anomalies

The registration of a marriage is an integral part of the solemnisation of marriage so was usually recorded at the time the event took place. However, if the incumbent did not make a return to the registrar on time to meet the quarterly returns then it will not be recorded in the right quarter. It may even completely miss being returned to the GRO because it was not picked up at the transmission of the next quarters marriages. Because a transcript is made for the GRO return there is always a chance that some information may be incorrectly transcribed.

Sometimes the index entries are only existent under just the name of the bride or the groom. If you do not know the name of one of the parties (usually the bride) then additional research is normally needed to confirm that you have found the correct marriage.

It is known that around 50% of marriage register entries contain errors or misleading information. Ages can be inaccurate and some were deliberate to avoid parental consent. Some will say "full age" when in fact, one or other party, or both, are a minor. It was quite normal in the Victorian period for the husband to be shown to be older than the wife and even if he wasn't then the parties recorded ages are adjusted to make it appear so. This can again be problematic for the uninitiated.

Names and occupations of fathers can also be inaccurate or misleading. Some parties, rather than give a father's name would provide information for the head of their household, guardian or perhaps step-father. In some registrations no name is given but it is wrong to automatically assume illegitimacy. Some clergy did not

18___   Marriage solemnized at_____ in the___ of___ in the County of___

No.	When Married	Name and Surname	Age	Condition	Rank or Profession	Residence at the time of Marriage	Father's Name and Surname	Rank or Profession of Father
38	18___		29	Bachelor	Miner	Cumberworth Oaks	George Lockwood	Dyer
			30	Widow			Robert Harry Cockhill	Weaver

Married in the_____ according to the Rites and Ceremonies of the Established Church, by___ or after___ by me.

This Marriage was solemnized between us: Herbert Lockwood / Emma Cockhill   in the presence of us: Thomas Tither / Joseph Wood

CERTIFIED to be a true copy of an entry in the certified copy of a register of Marriages in the Registration District of **Huddersfield**
Given at the GENERAL REGISTER OFFICE, under the Seal of the said Office, the 6th day of June 2003

MXB 306304

CAUTION: THERE ARE OFFENCES RELATING TO FALSIFYING OR ALTERING A CERTIFICATE AND USING OR POSSESSING A FALSE CERTIFICATE. ©CROWN COPYRIGHT

WARNING: A CERTIFICATE IS NOT EVIDENCE OF IDENTITY.

---

ask for the name of the father. Some people just invented a name to go onto the certificate and this really causes challenges if the name is unknown within your family research. Fathers names can be missing if they are deceased at the time of marriage and the absence of the word deceased alongside a name does not mean he was still alive at the time of the marriage. There is also no indication in a marriage certificate of whether a father is still at home or has deserted or divorced.

You may find, as I did, that information is incomplete on a certificate. I had a marriage certificate where the name of the parish, the date of marriage and the names of the parties were missing as was the method of marriage. Even the officiator had not signed the entry but because the "signatures" of the parties had been included the entry appeared in the GRO indexes

Marriages - a wider examination (not just of the civil registration period)

Many people come unstuck in researching a marriage. Whilst it was usual for a couple to get married before the birth of children many people have been known to get married at or around the same time that their first child was baptised. Marriages could also have taken place after the birth of some or all of the children so widening the search period is essential if a marriage eludes.

 The average age for people to marry was between 27 and 35yrs. Widening your searches based on age will more than likely reveal an elusive event.

Even in the Victorian period when supposedly high moral standards existed there is plenty of evidence suggesting that some couples never married. Statistics have shown that this could be as high as 1 in 20 relationships which were never formalised. Some marriages also took place in different countries so the use of supplementary indexes is needed. Border marriages such as those at Gretna Green of Coldstream are perfectly legal because they were subject to Scottish marriage law and the marriage is perfectly legal as it was solemnised across the border. Many couples travelled miles to participate in such ceremonies. If you cannot find a marriage then pursue this possibility.

Think also about clandestine (irregular) or "Fleet" marriages. A Fleet Marriage is an irregular or a clandestine marriage which took place before Hardwicks Marriage Act 1753 came into force on March 25, 1754. They were solemnised in or around London's Fleet Prison under the "Rules of the Fleet".)The earliest Fleet Marriage took place in 1613 although the earliest recorded in a Fleet Register was in 1674). As a prison, the Fleet was outside the jurisdiction of the church. During the 1740s, up to 6,000 marriages a year were taking place in the Fleet area, compared to around 45,000 in England as a whole which was quite a high proportion.

"Irregular" marriage still continued after the start of civil registration and was one that took place either away from the home parish of either the bride or the groom (but usually after banns or licence), or at an improper time. "Clandestine" marriages were those that took place away from a home parish, without either banns or marriage licence. Within English law, a marriage could be recognized as valid if each spouse had simply vowed to each other an unconditional consent to their marriage. These essentially are what is referred to as "common-law marriages". Nearly all marriages in England, including the "irregular" and "clandestine" ones, were legitimately performed by ordained clergy or legal clerks.

The scandals and abuses associated with clandestine marriages became the object of Lord Hardwicks Marriage Act 1753. This required that banns should be published or a licence obtained and that the marriage should be solemnized in church by a recognised clergyman. In the case of minors, it must also be with the consent of parent or guardian. Every marriage should be witnessed by at least two persons. Jewish and Quaker ceremonies were exempt from the act mainly because of the intricacies of recording such marriages within those denominations.

Marriages in other nonconformist chapels were no longer legal. Some staunch nonconformists however, did have marriage ceremonies in their own denominations and you would need to search minute books and other records of the particular denomination to find details. Some never "legally" married but were recognised as married in their own denomination. After Hardwick's Act, clergymen conducting clandestine marriages were liable to transportation but it is known that the marriage practice continued up to about 1770/1775.

After Hardwick many couples had to travel to Scotland, to places like Gretna Green or Coldstream. These had substantial use by the English until 1856, when

Scottish law was changed to require prior residency before a marriage could take place. In the Channel Islands, the 1753 Act did not apply.

Local tradition was also an important element of marriage. Not all marriages were legally constituted but families accepted that "jumping the broomstick" was equal in validity to having the "certificate". References to "broomstick marriages" emerged in England in the mid-to-late 18th century, always to describe a wedding ceremony of doubtful validity. In some communities it was the accepted way of marrying. It goes without saying therefore, that some such marriages will never be recorded but one important aspect is to establish whether your ancestors were part of such a community where this type of marriage was acceptable.

 Throughout the Victorian period around 1 in 20 couples never married formally. Look for records of local or ethnic group traditions if you cannot find a marriage. Before 1754 look at Clandestine marriages and after 1754 for nonconformists look at the minute books of the relevant denomination. Those who did not accept that they had to get married in the Church of England had a ceremony in their own denomination and considered it was all that was needed.

Death anomalies

It is strange how the use of death certificates is overlooked by many, some considering them to be unnecessary, however, they can contain as many gems as challenges. Ages at death can be notoriously inaccurate and in any case are only as good as the knowledge of the informant. Usually if a family member registers a death the age is generally accurate but someone else, be it a workhouse staff member, local nurse, neighbour or even a non-close relative they can be inaccurate. Age inflation was not unusual.

Occupations likewise are not always accurate. Many people are registered with a former occupation or the occupation description is elevated to make someone seem higher up the social scale than they really were. In most cases this is not a problem but family historians need to check the information out.

Many people are not concerned with cause of death and on early certificates before the cause was required to be certified, the causes of death are often singular and vague. Once certification was needed there is frequently more than one cause of death recorded. Today when more than one medical condition is recorded the first is the actual cause of death and the others are contributing factors or periods of time that the deceased had suffered from the contributing cause. Only the first entry is the cause of death, usually recorded as 1a.

Notification of death was usually required within five days of the event occurring. Deaths are recorded in the registration district in which they occurred, hence they may not be in your ancestors' home district. This is true of those dying in a hospital or other institution or whilst pursuing an activity away from home.

Additional Indexes for specific circumstances

There are several separate indexes to registers also held by the GRO which are worth a search when a challenge occurs and you cannot find the information in the normal indexes. Some are available and some are on application to the GRO.

The Thomas Coram register is a record of all children given into the care of the Foundling Hospital between 1853 to 1948. This requires application specifically to the Registrar General.

The adopted children register is a record of all adoptions granted by courts from the inception of the system in 1927 to present date. The original birth certificate is not taken out of the birth registration system so will still be available and is marked with the word "adopted" and initialled by the registrar but you will need the adopted name to find an adoption certificate in this index.

The still birth register is a record of all still births recorded from 1927 to present date.

Several series of regimental records are indexed for births/baptisms, marriages and some deaths relating to British Army regiments between 1761 and 1924. These are complemented by the chaplain returns which record the army chaplains' records of baptisms, marriages and deaths between 1796 and 1880. The army records relate to births, marriages and deaths of members of the British Army or their families, which took place abroad between 1881 to 1965 and are a follow on to the chaplains returns. The modern Armed Forces records also run to the present date.

Whilst looking at events abroad for British families there are also consular records of all births, marriages and deaths of British subjects registered at British Consulates commencing in 1849 to the present date, although it normally takes around a year for such events to reach the index system. Events registered by the British High Commissioners in other foreign countries exist from 1949.

Births and deaths at sea are recorded from 1837 to the present day in a separate index system. Marriages at sea were not legal.

Separate indexes cover deaths in the Boer war and both World wars covering the appropriate dates.

 In order to locate the reference for an overseas event you will need to look at the microfiche indexes available at Birmingham Library, Bridgend Local History Centre, Westminster Archives, Manchester, Newcastle and Plymouth Libraries or the British Library in London.

Census challenges

There is no doubt that searching for someone in the census returns is much easier online than it used to be when we had to trawl through endless microfilms without the aid of an index. However, it does not alter the fact that information may conflict or that people are missing or not where they "should be" in any particular census year.

The census is not altogether accurate, is not complete for the whole country, is rarely a complete record of all the family and does not provide all the information. At best it is a 10 year snap-shot of one night in the life of a family.

Illiteracy, language and dialect presented a challenge in recording the information correctly. Pet and nicknames were often used and you may only find the one forename they are known by recorded. In some institutions such as asylums and workhouses names are sometimes only recorded by initials for both forename and surname. Birth places, if correct, are often general rather than specific or recorded against the name of the nearest large town rather than the village or hamlet of residence. If the person was from "out of area" you may have to make do with just the name of a county or even country of birth. In fact, those not from the UK are recorded only by country because that was the instruction given to the enumerator to record in that way. Remember the census was a record completed according to government requirements at the time and not to help family historians.

From a research point of view, it is essential to know exactly when each census was taken and why some people may be missing from the returns. Familiarity with the process of taking the census is also recommended.

Using the census returns can be very positive in breaking through research challenges.

Age and birthplace can provide a vital clue particularly if the birth was before civil registration began. Birthplace information of family members will help trace mobility of the family. Wider family may be identified or a widowed parent may be resident with one of their children. They are a good occupational resource as many carrying out kindred occupations resided in the same neighbourhood, (railways, mines etc). Some temporary "villages" are also shown in one return and not another, such as those erected to house railway workers as they progressed with the construction extending the line (such as Jericho). These are very movable feasts but provide vital evidence of the movement of labourers, navvies etc.

The family's social status can be deduced by the number of servants they employed although some stretched their incomes to employ a general servant. The presence of step children can also provide clues which lead to researching earlier marriages particularly if both current and former wife shared the same forename. Step relationships and in-law relations are often interchangeable.

A word now on the use of indexes to locate a person or family. There are many inaccuracies on the indexes due to the way perhaps inexperienced indexers have interpreted names particularly capital letters at the start of a name. These anomalies present challenges which is an age-old problem and may even cause the more experienced researchers problems. Reading the many individual styles of enumerator handwriting is also a challenge. I recommend using the indexes on more than one website if you encounter difficulties in finding an ancestor, as each provider has worked their own indexes and the interpretation will be different and may even be correct on one of them!

To enable easier ways of finding entries try wildcard searches. Swap surname and forename around. Some indexers have actually indexed surname as forename and forename as surname when the enumerator has reversed the names in the entry. Try a search by using a forename alone with other known criteria such as age, place of birth, occupation. Don't use address unless it is in a village or small town. You can also search for other known members of the family because you do not know who else were resident on census night until you find the return. Very often you can uncover a family by searching on the wife's name as opposed to the husband. They are often referred to as the "head" when the husband is away working or they provided the information. Sometimes it is a good clue to a marriage breakdown.

A census is taken at an address, not specifically of a family or household so you could easily find more than one family in occupation.

When searching for your relatives, you should remember that even though your ancestor may have lived at one address, if he or she were not at home on the night of the census then they should not be included in the enumerator's records for that address. If they are reported by the head of the household as resident on the night, they may appear twice in the same census once at home and once where they were staying.

Many people, particularly young, unmarried women, were in service and may be found at the residence of their employers.

If for example you know that your ancestor was a sailor, he may have actually been at sea that evening - in which case he wouldn't be recorded on the census. However, if he was on a ship that was docked in an English port or serving with the Royal Navy, then he should be recorded at the ship's address when such returns were made. On some returns no provision was made to record seamen on ships at sea, only for those in port. In any case the Royal Navy was separately enumerated.

One major element which is overlooked by many in rural families is that because of the timing of the census many shepherds and other agricultural workers may well have been in a field hut somewhere tending the flock at lambing and may be missing from the census altogether.

Many of the enumerators - such as clergy - may have also recorded data about their individual parishioners from their own knowledge. On some entries data was so detailed that the enumerator even recorded how many dogs or hens certain parishioners had.

If you look at the disabilities column on the later census returns you may spot some instances where people were described as "lunatics", "idiots" or even "feeble minded"! The term idiot is generally applied to those who suffer from a congenital mental illness, and the term imbecile to persons who, in later life, have various stages of dementia or senility. The term lunatic is also frequently used with some vagueness, and probably persons suffering from idiocy, and suffering from dementia, were returned as such. It is known that those suffering from conditions such as Downs Syndrome, for example, were recorded as lunatics or idiots. Considering that many householders were illiterate and were being asked to give information about medical disabilities without any definition of the terms being used, the answers they gave should be treated with caution as they were not medically confirmed.

Once the 1881 census was fully compiled, officials noted that there was an alarming rise in the number of individuals being reported as "deaf and dumb", when compared to previous census returns. After enquiries were made, it transpired that many enumerators had recorded babies as being deaf and dumb simply because they were too young to speak!

There are missing pieces to several of the census returns for various years. FindMyPast has a very good listing of those areas affected. Perhaps the one which is most noticeable is the missing sections for the 1861 census covering areas of Middlesex, Kent, Sussex, Hampshire, Berkshire, Hertfordshire, Buckinghamshire, Oxfordshire, Northamptonshire, Cambridgeshire, Norfolk, Staffordshire, Worcestershire, West Yorkshire and large chunks of Wales.

In summary the anomalies on census returns can be grouped into:

Enumeration error – mishearing or being told incorrect information.

Refusal to complete a return – this was true particularly in 1911 when many families supported the Suffrage movement and refused to complete a return.

Pages missed in filming – like all filming there is a possibility of human error so check that the folio and page numbers for the village or street where you think someone may be living are consecutive. It is easy to turn two pages at once.

Houses physically missed by the enumerator – in courtyards, alleys, isolated rural areas.

Change of street name or numbering system – I have come across instances where a family appears to have been at four different addresses between 1841 and 1881 when in fact they were in the same house, it is just that the numbering changed as the street extended, and the name of the street changed twice during that time.

Institutionalised – many people would have been in hospitals/infirmaries, workhouses, prisons etc and may be recorded using only their initials rather than by name.

Many were in the armed services and abroad, on a ship or in a foreign country as the soldiers serving in the Boer war in 1901.

Travelling – itinerants, barge people, commercial travellers, train crew etc. may have been working away from home and enumerated elsewhere, if indeed they were enumerated. Some people may have been on holiday staying in a hotel and were not recorded at their home address. Sometimes property was recorded as unoccupied even if the residents were temporarily elsewhere.

Notwithstanding the challenges it is important, if you can, to find your ancestors on every available census and check the consistency of information. Do not rely on one census alone unless of course you have no choice. Using online searches may mean you actually have to think harder to find your family and as a final attempt you may need to resort to the old-fashioned searching through a microfilm. They are still available!

Always find your family in as many census returns as possible and fully analyse the findings to eliminate any anomalies and to make sure information is consistent. Doing this will open up a number of clues about the circumstances of the family throughout their lives.

Pre-1841 Census returns and population listings.

Census returns were made officially from 1801 so don't ignore pre-1841 census returns and other earlier population counts which may exist for the localities specific to your research.

The 1801 census asked local officials to provide information on the number of inhabited and uninhabited houses in the parish and how many families occupied them; the number of people in the parish and their employment; and numbers of baptisms, burials and marriages in the previous 100 years. A similar format was followed for the censuses of 1811, 1821 and 1831, with the addition of further questions.

Many of the early returns for 1801-1831 were destroyed with only statistical summaries being published. Those few returns that survive are now in the local County Record Office. The returns usually only name the householder and list the number of people in the house, although occasionally the whole population is listed.

The following information within the early returns may provide a valuable clue and as for later returns it is important to know when they were taken.

1801 - 10th March 1801

1811 - 27th May 1811

In 1811, the enumerators were asked to give more information about the reasons houses were unoccupied, so that the prosperity of the district could be more accurately gauged.

1821 - 28th May 1821

In 1821 a question relating to age was asked, in order to assess numbers of men able to bear arms, and to improve the tables on which life insurance was based.

1831 - 30th May 1831

More detailed questions on occupations from 1831 provided the government with economic information.

There may also be other earlier name-rich returns for specific areas. For example, in Bedfordshire there are "census" returns for the following areas:

Barton le Clay 1297, Cardington 1782, Hinwick 1778, 1788, Houghton Conquest 1712, 1833, Milton Ernest 1788, Pavenham 1699, Podington 1778, 1788, Renhold 1773, Southill 1833, Thurleigh 1788.

I would suggest searching your local archive catalogue to determine if earlier listings exist. You might not find many but you may also open a goldmine.

Just before the turn of the 19th century a listing was drawn up under the Defence of the Realm Act in 1798 of all able-bodied men between 15 and 60 yrs. not already engaged in military service. It was known as the Posse Comitatus and is an excellent research tool equal with the earlier census returns. Returns for counties are also held locally.

Parish register challenges

The parish register system was, over time, complex. It is important to know how, when and why registers existed at certain periods and how to interpret the information they contained. Generally, the earlier back in time you research the less information you will obtain from parish registers. Sometimes it is only a name and a date. The most infuriating entries are "Widow Smith" as a burial record!

The many variations in the way parish registers were completed seem to be a particular challenge. There was also some inventiveness with the use of nicknames given by the family between birth and baptism so the nickname or pet name is the name they were Christened with and it bears no resemblance to the name given at registration.

Another challenge relates to "family baptisms" where all the siblings gather together, usually in the parents' parish and have a "block baptism". This is great for identifying other family members but can be a challenge if that parish is some distance from where the family was living. It may mean that more than one child of a particular family are Christened together.

Adult baptisms also occurred and in some cases no indication exists in the entry that it is an adult being Christened. Because of the requirements under Canon Law sometimes this will take place prior to an Anglican Confirmation or prior to a church marriage where the persons infant/child baptism cannot be established or remembered. Of course, the person may not have been Christened as a child or perhaps converted later in life from another religious denomination. Many adult baptisms are therefore second baptisms. It is important to check otherwise the age and attribution can be distorted.

 Don't assume that all baptisms were performed as infants. Baptisms happened before confirmations or marriages and also when people changed their religious affiliations.

Block baptisms

Families often baptised their children together. I have seen baptism entries where eight or ten children have been baptised at the same time, usually after the birth of the youngest child. There are various reasons for this. Sometimes families forgot who they baptised so they did it again. Sometimes they were nonconformists and changed their religious affiliations having to rebaptise into the Anglican church (or vice-versa) revealing often a double baptism. It was not unusual in the larger towns and cities for a couple of children to be baptised together. It is also often a clue to a marriage. Not all couples married before the birth of some or all of their children.

Families moving in and out of nonconformity was not unusual and membership of a nonconformist religion usually required baptism on admission to that denomination.

Many illegitimate births took place in the workhouse infirmary. Because each workhouse had a chapel many children were baptised there as opposed to waiting until they were back in their own parish. This generally avoided embarrassment amongst the inhabitants of the village and did not enable the incumbent to include cryptic comments or suggest in the baptism register who the purported father was. Unfortunately, that does not help us! The birth/baptism registers of the workhouse need to be searched as an alternative to the parish baptism register if they have survived. You will need to check local archive catalogues to ascertain availability.

It is also important to remember that there may be more than one entry in a baptism register for the same infant and these are often no more than about six weeks apart. If a child was born and not likely to survive then the midwife or vicar would baptise in the home to enable a Christian burial if death occurred. This is often recorded in the parish baptism register as a private baptism. If that child survives then a further ceremony often took place accepting the child into the congregation and also for the churching of the mother after childbirth. Under normal conditions all this happens in the same ceremony for a healthy child and thus we only have one baptism entry.

Penny Marriages

Be aware of "penny marriages". These normally took place twice a year on Easter Sunday and Christmas Day. Many were "special offers" made by particular parishes and because of the volume of marriages the ceremony was a little unusual. Each couple made their vows independently but the rest of the service was a communal one. It is not unknown in such cases for marriage register entries on those two days to become mixed up. This would not always be identified as few couples were literate apart from perhaps being able to sign their name. Therefore, the wrong parties can easily be recorded against the marriage entry. This can be confusing when using marriage indexes and even in the GRO indexes. If your ancestors married on either of these days it is worth checking thoroughly the original marriage register if any doubt exists or looking to see if the name of the other party is recorded against another entry on the same day.

As a safeguard to researching a marriage ceremony, other supporting documents usually exist besides the actual register. Banns and licence entries (marriage allegations and bonds), a Bishops transcript (within the annual period), and a civil registration certificate. Marriages also had announcements or quite detailed reports in local newspapers, parish magazine or a workplace staff magazine. Whilst it is not always necessary to search all of these resources you will sometimes find alterations made to registers within the parish entry or by way of statutory declaration on the GRO certificate. As a minimum, if you suspect something is not quite right, you should look at both the GRO certificate and the parish marriage register entry.

Death and Burials

Many brick walls exist around death and burial particularly when you cannot locate either or your ancestor appears to have vanished. Remember that death and burial records capture more of the population than a birth/Christening entry or a marriage.

You may also have an ancestor who is recorded as "unknown" and this is true of someone dying whilst passing through a town or village in which they do not reside or are not known. This is also compounded by the number of bodies found in rivers, lakes and on the sea shore. Everyone of them has to be someone's relation but it becomes almost impossible to identify your ancestor in such circumstances. Rest assured that if your ancestor would be older than 110 years he or she is dead and therefore recorded somewhere.

One aspect which never ceases to amaze is that a burial for a female will be in the name that she was known as at the time of death. So, if your ancestor subsequently remarried after the death of a direct line husband then the burial will be recorded in her married name at the time of death. Although this seems obvious to the well informed you will be surprised how many family historians try to find a burial without first researching possible future marriages so remember there may be more than one subsequent marriage.

Wills and Probate

Wills and associated probate documents usually reveal much more about the personal lives and relationships of our ancestors than many other documents. They are especially valuable because of the genealogical information they provide.

Before the national civil system of proving a will came into force in 1858 Wills were proved by a number of ecclesiastical courts.

The Prerogative Court of Canterbury (PCC), which was held in London, was the senior church court, and dealt with the wills of relatively wealthy people living in the south of England and Wales. It also dealt with the estates of people who died at sea or abroad leaving personal property in England or Wales. During the Commonwealth period from 1653 to 1660, it was the only court able to deal with wills and administrations.

A useful research tool besides the PCC indexes is the National Wills Index which has a number of supplementary online indexes, abstracts and source documents. It includes all records proved in the Prerogative Court of York (PCY) which acted in a similar way to the PCC covering the north of the country, the British Record Society probate indexes and certain provincial wills including Oxfordshire and Chester as well as the Devon Wills Project, among others.

Up to 1782 every executor or administrator was required to send the court an inventory of the deceased's goods. The inventory itemised the moveable estate held by the deceased, but real estate was not included. These are a valuable resource indicating actual wealth of the testator. Only about 800 pre-1660 inventories have survived, but from 1660 to 1782 the coverage is much more comprehensive.

Most wills proved in the lower courts are held by Diocesan Record Office which for most of the country is the County Record Offices although that does not apply to every county. You should begin your search in the CRO that covers the area where your ancestor resided. There were over 300 pre-1858 church courts but don't let that put you off undertaking research as most have been consolidated into county-wide indexes.

Wills can often be difficult to read so you will need to understand old handwriting to identify and recognise common forms of letters, words and phrases. It is useful to make an extraction rather then read through endless legal jargon which does not affect the interpretation of the intent of the testator. There are basically ten points that you need to extract:

NAME of the testator
ADDRESS at the time the will was produced
OCCUPATION of testator
DATE will made –testator must have been alive
SIGNIFICANT PRE-AMBLE
BURIAL INSTRUCTIONS
NAMES & RELATIONSHIPS of beneficiaries, trustees etc.
PROPERTY (real and personal as bequeathed)
ATTACHED INVENTORIES OR CODICILS
EXECUTORS, TRUSTEES, WITNESSES

In regard to a search strategy for pre-1858 wills it is sensible to search the records of the local church court and work up to the higher church courts. By the early 19th century, many people proved the wills in the Prerogative Court of Canterbury as the business of the lower courts declined.

From 12th January 1858, the Civil system of proving wills and granting administrations began in England and Wales with the probate registry in London and district offices administering the system. Copies of all wills and administrations were lodged with the Principal Probate Registry. Today these are available electronically with indexes / calendars available online.

The records of the Death Duty registers where estate duty tax was levied on estates between 1796-1903 are an extremely useful supplementary resource. These accounts are useful in discovering extra information about the beneficiaries of wills or for supplementary information about the property of the testator. Often, they are "live" for about 50 years after the grant of probate.

The following valuable information can be found in the death duty registers which can also be used as a finding aid for where a will was proved.

The court in which a will was proved or an administration granted.

Information about the beneficiaries of the deceased's will (family relationships were often noted because close relations didn't have to pay duties on their inheritance)

The names, addresses and occupations of the executors
What happened to someone's personal estate (not freehold) after death
What the estate was worth, excluding debts and expenses
The name of the deceased, with address and last occupation
The date (as well as the place) of probate
Details of estates, legacies, trustees, legatees and annuities
The duty paid

Additionally, the following supplementary information often recorded in the entry will prove useful:

Date of death of spouse
Date of death or marriage of beneficiaries
Births of posthumous children and grandchildren
Change of address
References to law suits

Before 1812 the registers usually include very brief abstract of wills. From 1857 entries in death duty registers exist for all estates worth more than £20. However, those worth less than £1,500 didn't have the taxes collected and the register entries do not contain as much information as those of higher value.

Death Duty Registers can be a little complex to search but there are some good research guides at the National Archives where the documents are held.

OVERCOMING INADEQUATE RESEARCH

In the first instance I would venture that "gut feeling" has an important place in knowing if your research is correct or not. We supposedly fully understand our own family history and where we have reached in our research process. Very often we can assess whether the research does not look or feel right but now we have to prove it. In the first place it is recommended that you re-visit the original source of your information to make sure you have recorded information correctly and above all find out if you missed a vital clue. If you were a novice when you looked at the record originally then you could easily have made a misinterpretation of information or missed something.

These days it is easy to take a digital image of material but in the past, you may have recorded only the information in a document which you thought was relevant. Every piece of documentary information is relevant either now or may become so in the future. Don't ignore witness names, margin notes and other erroneous information that you see.

From here on in it is a matter of broadening your research simply from contiguous searches to widening the type and scope of records to research. Check and compare variations in details as you proceed, proving or eliminating as necessary.

Learn your boundaries – by this I mean that counties or villages do not have great big six-foot walls around them which are impassable to family movement. Just because you have found your family in one location does not mean that they did not move across the county or even parish boundary.

Above all question and verify for yourself each element of your research. **Check, check and if necessary check again.** Make certain that you have located the right person by working more than just a one-line pedigree. Branch out and work other family lines looking for a common denominator in your research. Go local – in other words visit the area on the ground and see for yourself what the town or village is like (remember however that environments change and it may look completely different today). You may also need to be aware of the terminology and language of the time as this could affect your results. Have street names changed, has the village vanished or been engulfed into a larger town? Above all remember illegitimacy – very few families do not have illegitimacy in their ancestry.

Part of the fool-proof process to overcome inadequate research is to:

1. Plan your research adequately

2. Follow the paper trail by using varied records

3. Stay focused looking for the answer to your goal only

4. Use a working pedigree to plot your research that way you live your research

5. Record in detail your source information as you need to know exactly what you research

6. Continually analyse your research as it is easy to miss something that may be very obvious

Live the research process

Planning your research is fundamental. Most of us will sub-consciously adopt the following process.

By reviewing what you know about an ancestor you will effectively be revisiting your existing research. Once reviewed you can determine what you want to find out based upon what you already know, whether it be a missing event, something about their occupation or life, a stay in hospital etc. Then comes the knowledge test and catalogue research because you need to locate suitable records that will provide the information. Make sure you are in the right place to find the information you are seeking. It is very frustrating and always a waste of time to visit the wrong archive but doubtless we have all done it. Once you have the record in front of you carry out your research and note everything down of relevance. Take a digital copy of the document for future reference. While researching ask yourself – does the information fit, is it what I want? If the answer is yes put the information into your working pedigree and go back to evaluating your information to enable you to take the next step. If it does not fit or is only a partial answer, locate another record and repeat the process.

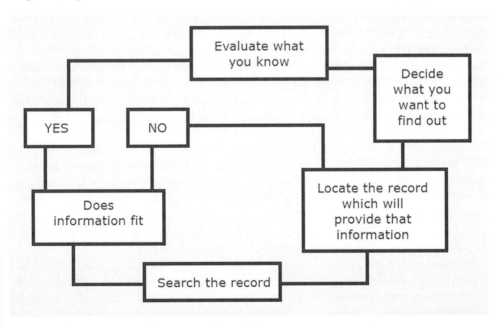

Picture your research

It is easy to review your research if you have a picture of it. Building a working pedigree will enable you to quickly and easily identify omissions, mistakes and improbabilities.

Looking at each individual and family will help you make sure that you have all the information that you want. You will be able to analyse easily – Do all dates fit? Is there an unaccounted-for gap? Are there any anomalies? Have you achieved all you set out to achieve with your research to date?

The beauty of a working pedigree is that it is a rough picture on which you can scribble all manner of notes to remind you to do something else. It is not a final presentation pedigree. Let me explain why I think a working pedigree is both important and extremely useful.

You are researching at the record office and have gathered loads of information which you have recorded in your notebook or perhaps on a spreadsheet on your computer. It is time for a coffee break or lunch and you want to review what you have found. Take the information from your notes and plot it onto your working pedigree. You then have a "picture" of your research and something tangible that enables you to analyse your new information as you progress your research.

By compiling your pedigree, you will identify any information that has not been found and above all indicate anomalies that need addressing. You can then address these before you leave the record office that day and avoid being frustrated at home when you start reviewing your notes and realise you do not have all the information you needed.

I recommend that you do this using paper but there is no hard and fast recommendations. If you choose to use a family history software programme on your laptop or tablet and enter information as you go you can still review your pedigree and determine missing information or anomalies in much the same way. Not quite as easy to include notes or jottings.

If you have never drawn a working pedigree there are a few simple protocols you can follow. Some of you may consider this is a little old fashioned but I believe it is fool-proof if you construct as you go.

Here's how to draw your working pedigree. I would suggest you use part of a roll of wallpaper lining paper (available at a modest price from any DIY store). You may also be able to use a sheet of A3 paper for the average family.

Start at the bottom of the sheet with youngest (nearest to you) generation in your research.

Divide your sheet horizontally into about four equal segments each representing a generation – that is probably more than enough for a day's research.

Always place the oldest sibling to the left side of your family line working to the youngest on the right-hand side of your pedigree chart. Allow enough space to add marriages or additional children you may yet find as your research progresses.

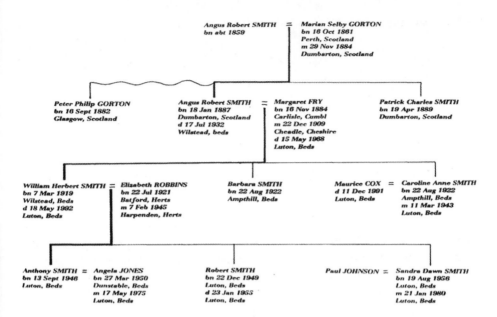

A marriage is always denoted by an = sign. For all marriages the males (grooms) are always recorded to the left of the equals sign. If you have females who possibly marry leave enough space to incorporate the husband on the left when you have located their marriage. Therefore, if you have a male child leave enough space on the right-hand side to note the wife and conversely if you have a female child leave space on the left to incorporate the husband. Remember also there may be more than one marriage.

The drop to the children of that marriage i.e. the later generation commences at the centre of the equals sign.

Leave enough space to enable additional siblings or second and subsequent marriages to be included. If you construct the pedigree properly then other marriages should be recorded in the right order with the first marriage on the left and second and subsequent marriages to the right. That way children of subsequent marriages also still appear in date order for the family as a whole.

The information recorded should ideally be basic data, birth, baptism, marriage, death, burial, will and occupation. You can however include whatever elements you wish but don't complicate the pedigree as this is a "picture" of your research not a full family history.

If you plot the chart correctly you can easily add missing children, marriages etc. but even if there is not enough room to do so on your main chart you can always draw supplementary smaller charts or include balloons with information in. Remember this is a working pedigree and not the final product. It does not matter what it looks like. As long as you understand what you have done and why, you will not go far wrong.

There are also a series of standard pedigree abbreviations which you may find useful and it would be worth getting used to using them as others throughout the genealogical world tend to adopt these. If you ever share a pedigree chart with others who are researching the same family lines then using standard abbreviations which are universally known avoids the possibility of any confusion in interpreting information. - However, few software programmes actually use these in today's world.

Timelines

Besides a working pedigree it is also useful to have a document timeline where you can identify what events influenced life and also to know, for example, when trade unions commenced or when a particular law was made resulting in a set of records.

There are four basic steps to creating a family history timeline

1. *Identify the Ancestor family you wish to plot.*
Ideally start with one ancestor family. There is nothing to stop you actually compiling this for each of your family lines but it will be best to work on one at a time in conjunction with your current research.

2. *Choose your software.*
There are several commercial software programmes available to the family historian for developing timelines. You can of course keep it simple by using Word or Excel spreadsheets or you can invest in mind mapping software or online software for creating timelines.

3. *Create Your Categories*
It's important to make sure all the important events including those that influenced your ancestor's life are recorded on your timeline. As you add categories to the timeline you will build up a picture of your ancestors' family in their contemporary environment. It will then become the start of their life story by putting their existence into context. We have already discussed records that will help you to do this so here is a brief recap in order that you do not miss anything.

Vital family information – births, baptisms, marriage/s, deaths and burials, not only of your ancestors' family but also for other relevant persons in their lives.

Life Highlights – in this category which will be the most extensive you should include, occupation/s, military service, land and property details, migration and emigration illness, institutions etc.

Regional & Local Events – these are events which only affect those living in a specific locality and would again very often reflect local political, social, economic and environmental influences.

World Events – many such events and happenings influenced how a family lived and were influenced by political, social, economic, medical and environmental history. Think about wars, epidemics, economic depressions, etc.

4. Identify Your Time Frame.

Before you start, identify the time frame you want to include. I would suggest you cover the whole period of your ancestors lives from the cradle to the grave (and beyond). You need to determine how you are going to record information, will it by decade, month or year. Any of these options help to focus your ancestors life. Will it also cover just an individual or all the family group members (parents and children). Using a timeline in conjunction with a working pedigree can really help to break down a brick wall as you are identifying a sequence of events in the life of your ancestor and overcoming the common challenges mentioned earlier.

 Having a visual family tree in front of you when researching reminds you of the information that you need to research before you leave a repository and enables you to determine if you have missed anything in your research.

Paper or Computer

Having previously indicated that it does not matter really whether you use paper or a computer/tablet in your research I would like to point out some of the possible pitfalls and advantages of using either.

Paper

- Focuses your research.
- A blank sheet of paper enables you to record everything without being restricted by the fields you have pre-set.
- Paper does not deteriorate easily.
- Is a hard copy record for future reference.
- Storage space/filing is a consideration. – I have many folders with my family history bulging from them!

Computer

Data entry using set fields in a spreadsheet, for example, may mean you miss vital information.

Computers / Hard drives can fail, "crash" or become corrupted causing loss of data unless you have backed up regularly. Most people who take computers to a record office do not back up data until they get home!

Data storage mediums will fail or be superseded by technology development. When I first started family history I used 5 ¼ floppy discs on an Amstrad 1512 computer. I have also broken a plug of a USB memory stick leaving the end in the computer USB socket and rendering the memory stick useless – so beware!

There are some record offices who do not allow the use of mains electricity so make sure your computer battery is fully charged and will last for the duration of your research.

You have no hard copy for future reference (unless you print out your research).

One final suggestion relating to picturing your research – Always take a copy of important information such as wills, etc. If using a digital camera make sure it is capable of photographing documents and use a steadying facility. There is nothing worse than getting home and finding that your copy is out of focus!

CLUES IN SECONDARY SOURCES OR SUPPLEMENTARY RECORDS

It is generally accepted within the realms of family history research that there are prime and secondary records available for research. It is frequently assumed, quite wrongly, that prime records are the only proven source of information. There is also a difference between secondary and supplementary sources.

To understand this more fully a definition is worthwhile. A primary source is any record created at the time of the event you are researching. Primary sources can include civil registration, personal letters, journals, tax lists, court documents, parish registers and parish chest records or a census (although enumeration books are compiled later).

A secondary source is a record created later by someone who did not experience the events that you are researching and can include Bishops transcripts, some probate records, published transcriptions, compiled databases etc. Most histories are secondary sources.

Sometimes a Bishop's Transcript of a register becomes a prime source if, for some reason, the parish register has not survived or is unreadable because of fading, damage etc. Often there is additional information recorded in the form of anecdotes in Bishop's Transcripts that are not in the original registers. I have even come across different names recorded in each record. I would however suggest looking at both, if both are available, and noting any different or additional information as this may be vital as your research progresses.

If something has sewn an element of doubt in your mind it is also recommended that you look, for example, at both a civil registration marriage certificate and also the parish register entry for the marriage.

Supplementary records relate to those which are related to the main event but do not form part of the prime record. These can include marriage banns or licence bonds and allegations and death duty registers, which in themselves are prime records but when you have established the existence of a will or administration and use them in conjunction therewith they are supplementary records.

Marriage banns can give vital clues about parish of residency and where a marriage is likely to have taken place. It also means a marriage should not have taken place before the date of the last publication. Equally there is no guarantee that the parties to the banns actually married. Marriage allegations and bonds can also confirm occupation, age (although may will just state "over 21yrs" or similar), father or guardian of the intended bride and the name of the person standing as surety which may or may not be a relative.

Using these types of documents very often uncovers clues to resolve research challenges.

Follow the paper trail

Many family historians are not fully aware of the number and variety of records which can be used to locate and find information about an ancestor or to confirm known or suspected detail. Irrespective of occupation or social group most people who have lived on this earth generated around 100 different records during their lifetime, most of which are available to research.

 In the resolve to find the elusive ancestor there are three fundamental steps to be followed: 1. Use every type of documentary evidence available, 2. Prove a connection before furthering your research, 3. Follow up and eliminate.

The following is a fairly comprehensive, but by no means exhaustive listing of such documents accompanied by suggestions about how to use them in your research to resolve a challenge. It is not a detailed synopsis of what the record contains or how to find it but to guide you to possible solutions to challenges. It is your responsibility as you search catalogues etc. to locate the most suitable record. It will therefore be up to you to use archive catalogues and research guides to locate records appropriate to your specific research.

The obvious and probably the most familiar are the documents of civil registration, census returns, parish registers and probate. There is a pre-conceived idea that some of our ancestors would not have left a will so we don't bother to look. Even agricultural labourers left wills so make a search for a will as automatic as looking at other records. These records have been previously discussed as the records present several challenges in their own right but are so valuable in locating an ancestor.

 The average ancestor, irrespective of social class, generated around 100 different documents during their lives (and just after) most of which are available to research and contain many vital family history clues to help resolve challenges.

Birth & Baptism

In some cases, it is necessary to go back and review the content of the family archive looking for mother's birthday book, the family bible, individual baptism certificate, the parish magazine where the family attended church or chapel and even an ancestors' diary notes.

Birthday book and family bible entries were usually done at or close to the event in question so are considered to be generally accurate. Parish magazines would normally have included a listing of the months' baptisms, marriages and funerals (or other events such as confirmations, Sunday school prize given etc). Many of these volumes have now found their way into local archives. Whilst they are not copies or transcripts of the entries in the parish registers they are an excellent finding aid.

Even looking at ephemera items like Christening spoons or cups may provide a date which can help further research.

In many family archives you are likely to find the "original" copy of a birth, marriage or death certificate for close family members.

The early years and education

School admission registers

Education records, no matter at what level, contain a wealth of information. School admission registers usually providing admission date, residence, date of birth or age and frequently the father's name and occupation, as well as previous school/s attended.

School log books usually give intricate detail about individuals, illnesses or reason for absence, movement etc. They can also give interesting insights into the social aspect of village or town life. The National School Admission registers and log books which cover the latter part of the 19th and early 20th centuries are very useful.

Examination certificates

Examination certificates and other education records are a good pointer to both the wealth of the family and also the academic standards achieved by a child ancestor. Many examination lists are also held by other institutions than the local archives such as school archives and organisations like the Girls Public Day School Trust. Even those who attended the National Board schools took "tests" in the subjects they learnt and these are very useful in determining literacy and education standards. School standard reports also indicate how well your ancestor was educated and can confirm whether he or she was literate.

Training Ships

One of the most challenging genealogical situations relates to "loosing a child". Records such as those of a child migrant or entry into a training ship can reveal some information of whereabouts. Training ships were used to train boys in all aspects of seamanship preparing them for a career at sea as well as providing secular education. Most boys went into training ships as a result of family involvement with the poor law system. Most then continued a career in either the Royal or Merchant Navy which was virtually guaranteed if you successfully graduated and wanted that type of career. If you have come across a "boy entrant" in the service record of your naval ancestor then a training ship record is a good place to begin research. For each boy that joined the training ship, the record books log the following: Name, Age, Date of admission and discharge, the parish or Poor Law Union from which they originated and what service the boy entered on discharge. You may also be lucky enough to find a copy of their Certificate of Competency, issued when they left the training ship, which will give a synopsis of standards achieved by the boy whilst in training.

University Alumni

University alumni or records of the Inns of Court reveal a potted history of anyone who matriculated. Every entry offers important information which may include any of the following: notable accomplishments, occupation, birth date, birth place, other schooling, spouse's name, parent's names, siblings and other important associations. Some ordinary and poor children were sent to universities under bursaries or scholarships so should not be ignored because it is felt that your ancestor is of the wrong social class to be a student. Students at some public schools such as Harrow were nominated by the Poor Law Authorities under the terms of establishment so ordinary working class boys did go to public schools.

Illness

None of our ancestors would have escaped illness during their lives and some would have fatal consequences.

Vaccination Records

Vaccination records are again a valuable set of records giving useful information. Mass vaccination programmes took place and records exist of compulsory vaccination against smallpox. Widespread vaccination of children began in the 1830s with the passing of the first Vaccination Act which was administered by the Poor Law Unions. However, vaccination was voluntary and take-up was so poor that vaccination became compulsory in 1853 under an amended Act stipulating that parents must vaccinate their children within three months of birth. Vaccination registers were kept by local registrars and a vaccination certificate was issued to the parents of each vaccinated child.

A further Act in 1867 strengthened the legislation and handed responsibility to the Poor Law Guardians resulting in 1871 of the appointment of district vaccination officers. The officers were usually medical officers from the workhouses who assumed responsibility for keeping the records. Half-yearly registers were submitted by the registrar to the vaccination officer showing the newly born that had not been vaccinated. The vaccination officer also held the 'Return of Deaths of Infants under Twelve Months of Age' which contains the child's full name, the date and place of death and the father's name and occupation or the mother's name if the child was illegitimate. Parents were often prosecuted for non-compliance. Annotations were included in the vaccination registers of those who refused. Prosecutions were usually administered by the Quarter or Petty Session Courts. These records are a very useful source for confirming or even locating births and infant deaths thus helping to locate missing children. Certificates, where they are available, contain similar information that could be found on a normal civil registration birth certificate but do not always give the mother's name. Compulsory vaccination was abolished in 1949. Some of these records may lurk in family archives.

Hospital Records

Hospital admission registers and patient records can also be quite revealing. Patient case records show a great deal of detail which, although time restricted, may have an indication of a lifelong disability which affected work or family relationships. Infirmary admission records are a valuable tool in breaking through challenges. Many will give dates and places of birth as a starter.

Baptisms sometimes took place at lying-in (maternity) hospitals which were established in the 18th century. Giving birth in general hospitals only became common practice with the establishment of the NHS. Before World War II, the majority of women gave birth at home and in places like workhouse infirmaries or cottage/charity hospitals. Some hospitals might have records of a baptism which took place within hospital chapels. The use of such records for births and baptism should not be overlooked.

Patient records for adults aged 16 and over are closed for 84 years from the date of the record. For children between the ages of seven and fifteen closure is for 93 years and for infants up to six years old closure remains for 100 years. In practice those records held by archives can often be made available on production of a death certificate for the appropriate person. It does not mean that you will actually see the record but often archivists are prepared to either copy or extract the information relating to the individual rather than produce the whole volume of documentation. If the record is in the form of a separate file you should be able to see a copy but the over-riding decision rests with the archives as to availability.

Hospital post mortem records

In the event of deaths in a hospital and the need for a post mortem the hospital post mortem records will provide more information than can be found on a death certificate often giving a detailed insight into a reason for a death. They may not survive for all hospitals and may be full of medical jargon. If patient records don't survive you may be able to find post mortem registers providing basic information.

Asylum Records

If you are unlucky enough to find that your missing ancestor was committed to an asylum and the reasoning behind such admission sometimes defies modern logic, then again asylum admission registers and patient notes can be extremely revealing. Most will provide intricate detail and a physical description of the patient.

Before the establishment of specialist asylums, those considered to be lunatics were housed in charity hospitals, workhouse infirmaries and sometimes county gaols. The wealthier members of society would also section their family members (usually wives) to private asylums for such things as withdrawal of conjugal rights or other actions which were against the will of the husband.

The majority of county asylums were built following the 1808 County Asylums Act. Not every county had an asylum until the passing of the 1845 County Asylum

Act which required at least one asylum for every county. Although provision now existed for the mentally ill many individuals were still sent to the workhouse. At this time as well, the Lunacy Commission was set up to oversee the welfare of mentally ill patients and to regulate admissions which it did not always do.

Think also about criminal lunatics and admissions to places like Broadmoor and the Bethlem Asylums which were used nationally. The first port of call for such research would be court records. Asylums were an alternative (and often harsher punishment) than prison.

Probably the most useful and widely available asylum records are the admission registers which show both admission and discharge of patients, often within a short space of time. Asylum records are subject to a 100 years closure but can usually be accessed by family members. In many such records it is not uncommon to only find a forename recorded in the registers. Patient records, where they are available, are a goldmine of information because they contain almost a diary of events, medications and treatments, demeanour and characteristics. Another valuable piece of information is that the crown took custody of lands and property belonging to lunatics although you need to be aware of implications of the Married Women's Property Act.

First World War Field Hospital Records

One of the most pertinent set of records in the early 20th century are the records generated by the Field Hospital system which operated during the First World War. Many who served, and if they were not killed, were wounded, some being treated at the front, some sent home to convalesce and some returned to their unit after treatment. The Field Hospital system provided care and treatment at various levels and the records will be revealing showing unit, rank, period of service, patient details and transfers. These are useful as a supplement to any available service record and certainly a vital resource in the event of a service record not surviving. There was an established evacuation chain for wounded and sick soldiers. A casualty would have received initial medical attention at first-aid posts situated on or close behind front-line positions. The units in the trenches generally had a Medical Officer, orderlies and men trained as stretcher bearers who would provide support. They would transport men to Field Ambulances. This was a mobile medical unit, not a vehicle. Each army division had three such units, as well as a specialist medical sanitary unit. Field Ambulances also established Forward Dressing Stations where a casualty could receive further treatment so he could be evacuated to a Casualty Clearing Station. Men who were ill or injured would also be sent to the Dressing Stations and in many cases returned to their unit after treatment. The Dressing Stations were generally manned by the Field Ambulances of the Royal Army Medical Corps.

Once treated at a Dressing Station, casualties could be moved rearward several miles to the Casualty Clearing Station.

The Casualty Clearing Station was a large, well-equipped and static medical facility. Its role was to retain all serious cases that were unfit for further travel, to treat and return slight cases to their unit and evacuate all others to Base Hospitals. Casualties would normally be moved from the CCS to a Base Hospital by specially-fitted ambulance trains or in some circumstances by ambulance barge along a canal.

Most Field Hospital system records provide valuable information: Surname, normally only Initials of forename, rank, regimental number, sometimes the regiment and battalion, age, and length of service, Details of the sickness/wounds incurred (including severity and location on the body). This information was frequently in Field Ambulance records where triage took place. They could also include medical establishments transferred from and to and any repatriation to the UK – useful if a soldier was sent to a remote area of the country away from his home location which was frequently the case.

Patient notes often included such information as whether the wound was or could have been self-inflicted (some soldiers tried this to escape service), whether a court martial was referred to and if a wound stripe was awarded.

These records are a really valuable resource for those where no other personal records have survived. They can also enhance existing information about an individuals' service life where other records do exist. Most units also maintained War Diaries which, although mainly administrative, do frequently give information about men treated and moved on. For the early 20th century they can be a really useful research challenge breaker. However the records which exist are only a representative selection so beware you may not find what you are looking for.

Working Life

There are many records relating to the working life of ancestors and because most are not classed as public records tend to be a neglected source of information. Most people worked from an early age, sometimes as early as 5 or 8 years until they could no longer work. The old age pension did not come into existence until just before the First World War.

We will discuss occupational records later but just to whet your appetite and set you thinking, the following is a list of some of the records available to research, some of which exist in private archives. Many family historians ignore these, possibly through ignorance of their existence.

Apprenticeship records

Apprenticeship records were maintained by the poor law authorities, were privately taken out or issued under the jurisdiction of livery companies and trade guilds. Records can include registers, indentures and binding books. Many children were also apprenticed to their father or uncle. What happened at the end of an apprenticeship? – a freedom certificate may well have been presented. There are also apprenticeship tax records.

The main surviving records are the registers kept by the Inland Revenue following the Stamp Duty Act and cover approximately 100 years from 1710 to around 1815. The Act imposed a levy on apprenticeship agreements and centralised the registry of indentures. If the tax was paid in London (irrespective of where the master lived) then the entries were recorded in the city or town registers but if the tax was paid in the regions then the entries were recorded in the country registers. Interestingly, the city registers could include entries from the whole of England but especially Middlesex and the home counties as well as for Wales and Scotland. The Act did not apply to parish or charity sponsored apprenticeship agreements or those where the fee was less than one shilling. (The registers in series IR 1 at the National Archives and are arranged chronologically within the areas). Indexes are available at the Society of Genealogists, the Guildhall Library and online.

Overseers of the poor were required to keep registers of apprentices under the 1801 Act and these, where they exist, are included in the parish chest records. They can provide a wealth of information to help resolve a challenge and include the name, address and occupation of the master as well as information about the apprentice which can include age/date of birth, location and father or guardians name. Such detail can supplement primary record information or provide information previously unknown.

Apprenticeship records were also kept in the Court books of the London Livery Companies and trade guilds throughout the country. The Statute of Artificers and Apprentices between 1563 and 1814 regulated the apprenticeship system which stipulated that an apprentice must serve at least seven years before practicing his trade. They had to be over the age of 10 but under 18 and be the son of a freeman.

Actual indentures seldom survive and those that do are mainly in the family archive or in private hands. Some of the larger company archives and Livery Company records include the actual indentures. It seems that many instigated before 1710 no longer exist. Also, the apprenticeships between father and son or other relative usually had no formal indenture. Even after the Stamp Duty Act many did not pay the premium tax and are therefore unrecorded because certain trades and occupations were not subject to the apprenticeship system.

If your ancestor was a military serviceman look at the records of the King's Freemen which relate to discharged servicemen given special privileges to trade in any town and city throughout Britain. Those given the right to trade were not officially Freemen but merely granted the right by the Crown. Such rights were also granted to the man's wife and children. The records contain the man's discharge papers, marriage and baptism certificates for the wives and children and cover the period from around 1749 to 1816.

All of these records have high genealogical value as they include: Master's name, address and occupation, the name and address of the apprentice, name, parish, address and occupation of apprentice's father or guardian (if a mother is given it is a strong clue that the father is deceased or that the apprentice was illegitimate), and details of the terms of the agreement which tended to be fairly standard throughout.

The Merchant Navy also had a strong contingent of apprenticeships. The

Merchant Shipping Act 1823 required all ships over 80 tons to carry at least one apprentice. The legal documents binding an apprentice to the ships Master were required to be filed with the Customs Officers in the ports at which the apprentice was enrolled. After 1835 all London enrolled apprenticeships were registered with the Registrar General of Shipping and Seamen. Many apprentices did not complete their term or else did not complete it with the same Master.

Trade directories

Those who then followed their own trade, skill or occupation may well appear in trade directories, poll books and electoral registers.

One of the most important and comprehensive resources for researching tradesmen is a local trade directory. Trade directories enable us to piece together our ancestors' lives. As well as listing the gentry, clergy, professional people, merchants and tradesmen they are time capsules providing snapshots of contemporary environment, work and culture.

The resources provide peoples locations, can narrow down someone's death, and when they moved or retired.

The first known directory was Lee's 1677 Directory of London Merchants, followed by a further series for London and other major UK cities mostly from the 1700s. Directories became abundant in the 19th century with the first series published by Pigot between 1814 and 1853, and then by Kelly from the mid-1830s. Most of these also include brief histories and descriptions of each parish or town. Remember by their sheer nature the information would be history before publication as they were often compiled 6 - 9 months earlier.

Employment service records

The information available in employment records can reveal some interesting facts about your ancestor and may well provide vital clues to movement. In some cases you will even find the CV, employment contract and details of wages paid, promotions etc. These records are extremely useful to trace the locations of an ancestor throughout their working life. They should not be used in isolation but alongside other records of employment.

Agricultural estate records

Amongst the working classes mention may exist in estate records, log books of farms, wage records and diaries. Those who were employed as servants did not, for a period, escape the male and female servants tax and should be named alongside the employer.

Many agricultural labourers worked for large estate owners or their tenant farmers and as such will appear in the journals and wage records kept by the estate. The secret is to know who they worked for and resources which help determine this should be the first port of call including the Victoria County Histories, which frequently indicate manors and large landowners.

Documents relating to the administration of an estate include plans, accounts, terriers, rentals, valuations, surveys, leases, deeds, maps and correspondence. Many villages (known as "Closed" villages) were controlled by an estate owning family. Estate maps show the extent of estate lands which may include detached areas in different parishes thus providing a clue in regard to locality of residence or work. The amount of detail varies and could include every dwelling and building or just the boundary, paths and key landmarks. As landowners often held estates in different parts of the country it was not unusual for estate workers to be transferred and records to be held in only one archive.

In early periods (pre 1850) it is worth investigating information in manorial records.

Trade union records

Anyone who worked in industry would have belonged to a trade union and the records of many are available for research both for the local branch and the national records.

This is a much under-used source of valuable information. The scale of the British trade union movement suggests that hundreds of thousands of workers have been members, and around 5,000 trade unions are known to have existed, although many are now amalgamated into the major unions of today.

The amount of detail in each unions' records can vary depending on the record type and what the union chose to record. Many will include a combination of the following: name, birth year, admission year and age, trade union branch, any transfers, offices held etc.

Most Unions maintained Quarterly membership returns, which included subscription details and benefits paid. The admission books are possibly the most valuable as they include items like length of time in the trade, marital status, and sometimes a date, dates of death or any exclusion from the union. The Registration books give similar information.

Many records are held by the Modern Records Centre at the University of Warwick. Some Trade Union Branch records may be held locally and it is always worth looking at the provincial newspapers as many reported on the happenings at local trade union branch meetings and may mention ordinary members who perhaps served on committees of raised issues, made comments etc.

Trade and staff magazines

There are many specialist trade journals held by the British Newspaper Library, some of which are already available on the British Newspaper Archive web site. Staff magazines will provide further details about an ancestor particularly records of promotions, retirement, sporting achievements and sometimes even engagements and marriages. Railway companies, the Post Office and many of the larger industrial concerns like Bata published these on a regular basis.

Professional year books and membership records

Those who have ancestors who entered the professions have access to a series of year books and directories as well as possibly finding information about achievements, branch membership, appointments etc. Virtually every profession published such material and many professional bodies also kept detailed membership applications and records about the individual and where they were employed. Most of these are still held by the professional bodies who generally have their own archives.

The Public Face

Newspapers

With the advent of online material, it has become much easier to search newspaper records for details of your ancestor. Please note that all newspapers are not online but there are various sites to research. Some national newspapers such as the Times and Daily Mirror have their own websites allowing access to digitised images of past and current publications. You may have to subscribe. Some of this will be an unwelcome intrusion into their lives, some will reveal that your ancestor was a criminal (you may not even know that) and some because of heroic achievements etc. Newspaper reports of a marriage or funeral can list relatives attending (with a note of actual relationships), family photographs may well be included which you knew nothing about.

There are many reasons that a newspaper can be helpful in resolving family history challenges but you also need to be careful. The late nineteenth century was the heyday of the newspaper and local papers flourished, many for only short periods of time. Historic newspapers were often only 4 - 6 pages long and unlike modern papers carried advertisements and notices on the front page rather than a headline story. While you will find some wonderful engravings particularly as part of advertisements, there were few photographs until after 1910. The expense of producing the newspaper meant that the text is often densely packed to make the most of the available space, there are few headlines and each story is followed closely by the next. Many provincial newspapers also lifted stories from other papers and to some extent this may not be current news.

To get the most out of a local newspaper don't restrict yourself to one local paper. Newspapers printed stories from all over the country so it is not unusual to find a story from Scotland published in a local paper from Bedfordshire.

When undertaking an online search use surnames. In the 19th century first names were not always published. Your ancestor could be known as "Smith", or "a young man called Smith". Newspapers are searchable from an index using Optical Character Recognition and fuzzy or blurred print can make it difficult for the computer to translate the text. Keep this in mind when searching as very often index searches return gobbledegook. Luckily several newspapers will often report on the same event and use the same generic script so it may be easier to find in some than others.

Some of the language used can be unfamiliar and the names by which we know a historical event might not be the name used to describe it when it happened. The classic relates to wars – The Boer War was often wrongly referred to as the Zulu War and World War One was referred to as the Great War.

Newspapers are most valuable for the following:

Hatch, Match & Despatch notices (birth, marriage & death) which appeared regularly after 1820 and also include announcements about family members who have moved abroad or who became engaged to be married. Very often these are on the same page and in the same column for every edition of the newspaper.

If your ancestor was in the civil service or military services, their promotions and movements are frequently recorded and can be followed in the local newspapers. Unfortunately, this rarely applies to non-commissioned officers of the armed forces. The official Gazettes are the way forward on this.

Story-like advertisements can give you great insight into your ancestor's business dealings.

Reports of bankruptsy and insolvent debtors including names and addresses of borrowers and money-lenders were usually printed in newspapers as were court reports. These feature regularly in newspapers and contain the names of defendants, victims and witnesses. Court reports often provide physical descriptions of defendants, intricate details of the circumstances (which don't always appear in official records) and report testimonies, allowing you to "experience" your ancestor's voice.

You will find long lists of names in the newspapers acknowledging contributions to charity and group membership, together with the minutes of public meetings giving names of the committee or council members.

Specialist papers and magazines can also help you find details of your ancestor. Sports newspapers are excellent for tracing athletic ancestors, football match results and match reports and even the local darts team achievements were reported. There were also specialist newspapers for stage and theatre so if your ancestor was associated with the stage either professionally or as an amateur then you may find information about them and the shows/concerts they staged. Various movements such as the Suffragettes published their own newspaper so again if your ancestor was involved they may well be mentioned in those papers particularly if they were prominent in either the local or national bodies.

For those with seafaring ancestors Lloyd's List is an essential resource. This newspaper reported on the movement of ships whose home ports were in the UK and Ireland and very often mentions names of individuals including passengers of banana boats and other merchant shipping when they arrived at their destination port.

The Poor Law Union Gazette is a rich resource for family historians, particularly for those where families were broken up by poverty and finding a deserting ancestor becomes a challenge. The paper publishes notices of men and women who absconded from their families using workhouse admission as the means of desertion. Details include names, last known whereabouts and physical descriptions. Such a record will inevitably give vital clues about possible bigamous marriages or suggest the existence of a second family elsewhere.

Historical newspapers print details that would not be included in modern newspaper reports. The details of events can be quite graphic. Incidents such as suicides were reported with full details such as the name of the person and the circumstances of their death.

Correspondence for public office

Maybe your ancestor stood for public office or campaigned for a local cause. Such records, often in the form of correspondence, can add flesh to the bones and also help you to overcome research challenges because of the golden clues you can find by researching records of elections, council meetings etc.

Society, Club and Association records

Friendly Society, Benefit Societies, Sporting Clubs and Allotment Association records, even if only a subscription book, can show what aspects of public life your ancestor was involved in. Inevitably there will be photographs in local papers or official records which will show your ancestor in his or her true light. Various membership records of non-political mutual societies established to assist members financially in time of illness, old age and hardship exist in local record offices. They were funded and governed by their members and included friendly societies, building societies, loan societies, industrial and provident societies.

By law Society rulebooks had to be submitted to the Registrar and these are now available at The National Archives. Some earlier formed societies deposited their rulebooks with the Quarter Sessions and as such they will be held locally. The annual reports produced by the Registrar from 1852 are found in the Parliamentary Papers. These in themselves may not be particularly valuable except to locate a particular society, if for example, you have a note of the name of a society that your ancestor belonged to. From the late 17th century many societies operated purely along fraternal social lines or as charitable institutions. Also, consider looking for the women and juvenile branches of a friendly society. The name of the organisation did not necessarily indicate the occupation of its members. The records provide challenge breaking information in the form of name, occupation, place of birth, address, age, meeting places, date of death.

Serving King and Country

Virtually everyone will find ancestors who served in the military or navy, including the local militia. The records generated by the administering bodies should not be neglected as a source of information. They will include service records, operational records and administration records. Most of us will have personal knowledge of those of our family who served in the two World Wars and perhaps the Boer War but during Queen Victoria's time the British fought in many different wars or skirmishes. Go earlier and we have the Napoleonic Wars and even earlier the hundred years war, civil war etc. Many of our ancestors would have spent prolonged periods abroad whilst in the armed services. Some never returned home and chose to live the rest of their lives in foreign climes. Many served prolonged periods in places like India, often marrying locally and bringing up children in those countries.

Maybe we are familiar with the content of army or navy service records, but what about other material that can provide a wealth of information about our ancestor whether he was an officer, non-commissioned officer or other rank. Service records for everyone who served do not exist, particularly in the army, so, irrespective of whichever service your ancestor served in, looking at supplemental materials can help break through the research challenge.

Medal Rolls

Since the creation of medals every serviceman awarded either a campaign medal or a gallantry or long service/good conduct medal has been recorded. Many are indexed but research of the medal roll will provide useful information. You will also need to know which period medals covered. Unfortunately, families had the habit of disposing of medals when the recipient died.

One large misconception exists around the First World War army medal rolls. The index cards you readily view online are not the original medal roll and whilst the index card provides useful information, the key is in the reference to the roll and page and it is always worth looking at the actual roll itself. Some index cards include gallantry awards but most relate to campaign medals. One of the most useful aspects of the index card is the record of different regiments your ancestor served in, together with the service number for that regiment. However, few give the battalion so it is difficult to look at other material such as war diaries etc. The key to whether you will find a medal award depends on whether the unit in which they served was in an operational theatre. Some who served only at home were not entitled to medals.

WWI medals are inscribed around the rim with the soldier's surname with first name or initial, rank, regiment and service number. Medals from World War II and campaigns from the 19th century such as the Crimean War are not inscribed with this information. Check also in both local and national newspapers for reports of a gallantry medal award.

Navy and Royal Marine medals are recorded for both Ratings & Officers. For World War I, the rolls include most of those who saw active service overseas. They are compiled for the various divisions of the Navy which existed at the time. There were three types of medals awarded to those serving in the Royal Navy namely; Campaign, Gallantry and Good Conduct or Long Service.

The Naval General Service Medal was initiated in 1847 and retrospectively covered the years from 1793 to 1840. These include, the French Revolutionary Wars, the Napoleonic Wars, and the Anglo-American War of 1812. There are in fact two series, the second series covering 1915-1962. This medal series was instituted in 1915 to recognise service by personnel serving with the Royal Navy and Royal Marines in minor naval operations that would not normally attract a specific campaign medal. The Army and Royal Air Force equivalent was the General Service Medal. In 1962 both these medals were replaced by the General Service Medal and issued for all campaigns across the services.

The Long Service and Good Conduct Medal was instituted in 1833 and issued to other ranks and NCOs for long service with good character and conduct.

Don't forget the Silver War Badge records from 1916. The Silver War Badge was issued to officers and soldiers discharged or retired from the military as a result of sickness or injury at home or overseas during the First World War. The award is particularly useful as recipients had not necessarily served overseas and would therefore not have been awarded a campaign medal. The award provided the recipient with a public means of showing that he had been honourably discharged and was accompanied by a certificate which may well be found amongst family archive papers.

Commission Warrants

If your ancestor was an officer you may well find details of his commission warrant (a personal document) or details of how much was paid for a commission in the army. There are however many administrative resources which will record commissions including those army commissions which were purchased and sold. Commissions in the Navy were subject to stringent examination and also depended upon seniority with officers moving up when a vacancy occurred. Those for the army were purchased and sold with only some exceptions. The cost involved depended upon the rank purchased and the prestige of a particular regiment. It was more expensive to buy a commission in the guards than infantry for example. Only commissions in cavalry and infantry regiments could be purchased and only up to the rank of Colonel. Commissions in the Royal Engineers and the Royal Artillery were awarded to those who graduated from the Royal Military Academy, Woolwich, and subsequent promotion was by seniority. The purchase of commissions was abolished as part of the 1871 Caldwell reforms, after which it was awarded on merit and training at schools like Sandhurst.

For both services don't forget the difference between commissioned and non-commissioned officers.

Pay Lists and Musters

Both the army and the navy (including their various divisions) generated pay lists and musters listing details of all their men. They cover initial recruitment/ enlistment, their service and details as they became non-effective (left the service), following which pension records need to be researched. Valuable information can be found in these lists for the sake of spending some time in research such as; those killed may well have a record of effects, did sailors receive prize money in the Navy? Were they prisoners of war? Did they leave a diary which may well exist in a record office or military/naval museum if not in a family archive?

To trace a man's army career by way of the musters, you will have to know the name of his regiment and battalion. Some musters exist from c1708 but the majority are from 1730 to 1898. From 1888 onwards, there are only muster rolls because pay lists were discontinued at that time and by 1898 muster rolls were no longer kept by the War Office either.

Description books contain a description of each soldier, his age, place of birth, physical description, trade and service, and are organised by regiment. These books are in alphabetical order of soldiers' names and cover roughly 1756 to 1900. However, for many regiments they only cover the first half of the nineteenth century.

During the Crimean War, men were recruited abroad to form the British German Legion, the British Italian Legion, and the British Swiss Legion. These forces were formed as a result of the Enlistment of Foreigners Act 1854 and they became known collectively as the British Foreign Legion. A total of 14,000 men were recruited most of whom never saw active service and all Legions were disbanded after the war.

Musters and pay books for the Royal Navy are organised differently. It is necessary to know the name of the ship on which an ancestor served. Before 1853 using this type of record is the only way of tracing a man's career (unless they were officers when using the Navy Lists is important). There are various series of pay lists and musters so make sure you have the right document for the purpose of your search (see My Ancestor was in the Royal Navy). Records in this class end in 1878 so there is an initial overlap with continuous service records.

Disposition of the British Army

There are many ways to find out locations at which a regiment was stationed. The Disposition books are in a little used resource of WO379 at TNA covering 1737 - 1967. Using this source will enable you to piece together the locations of the regiments in which your ancestor served. More laborious methods include tracking through the muster rolls, army lists or station lists published in newspapers or by using "In Search of the Forlorn Hope".

Museums

One really neglected source of information, frequently for background information or history is the Regimental or Navy museum. These very often have information directly relating to an ancestor or detailed histories of his battalion or ship. I have visited such and come away with a wealth of information about my ancestor. Sometimes medals or personal diaries/papers have been presented to the museum by next of kin which can be photographed.

Service records

One final word on service records. Those who served after 1923 and whose records survive are held by the appropriate service records department. You can gain access on payment of a statutory fee but some information may be redacted if you are not a close relation. It should also be re-iterated that those leaving the Navy or Marines at the end of World War two were given the option of taking their service record with them so you may find the Navy no longer have a record of your ancestor.

The British Abroad

Passports

Although the majority of travellers abroad did not require a passport or licence to pass beyond the sea many did obtain one, particularly those who travelled on official business or were merchants. Those who emigrated did not need such documentation but there are many documents available to trace emigration.

The earliest British passport was issued in 1414 either by Act of Parliament or by the Privy Council. From 1778 most were written in French so be prepared to translate if you find one for your ancestor. It was not until 1915 that the "modern" style of passport with photograph and signature was instigated. Before the First World War it was not compulsory for someone travelling abroad to apply for a passport. There are online indexes to passport holders between 1851 and 1916 with gaps for 1857 and for the period 1863-1873. Registers of passport applications were compiled by the Foreign Office and are available between 1795 and 1948.

Merchant Company records

Because of trading organisations such as the East India Company, The Hudson Bay Company and the South Sea Company many British citizens have lived for prolonged periods of time in foreign climes. Many would have married and raised a family in their destination country. Records of birth/baptism, marriage, death/burial and probate have been generated particularly in India and some areas of the Far East. Using these records will fill in many gaps in our ancestry.

India, for example, had a complete administration system recording birth and baptism, marriage, military and civil service, death and probate together with loads of information about qualifications, training and service within the East India Company. If you have "lost" an ancestor even for a short period then consider records of the various merchant companies at home or abroad. These records are mainly in the form of returns sent back to England and some never made it or were lost on route so not every record survives. This is true of the India birth, marriage and death records where it is known that the series is incomplete.

Like any employer, the EIC needed information to enable them to recruit suitable people and to manage them once they were in post. Various records of employment exist. They also documented their financial obligations, such as the payment of pensions. As a result of their careful record-keeping, we can find out a wealth of fascinating details about people from all walks of life who were living and working in the Indian subcontinent.

Of particular interest may be the staff employed on railways. The EIC particularly, but not solely, seconded staff from the British railway companies to go and work in India for periods of time and many also left the British rail companies to work abroad. This was particularly true of footplatemen and also permanent way crews. Many returned to their original UK posts on completion of their contracts.

The records of the East India Company are vast, to the extent that much of the Asia and Africa Studies Section of the British Library is devoted to the archive. There are also excellent guides and databases to help with research.

The South Sea Company was founded in 1711 to trade with Spanish America, on the assumption that the War of the Spanish Succession would end with a treaty permitting such trade. The British Library, London, holds records of the South Sea Company, 1711-1856 but some records are held by the City of London Joint Archive Service.

As you would expect the main records of the Hudson Bay Company are held by Manitoba Archives and include name indexes, servant contracts and other staff/employee records, many of whom were British or had British origins. Biographical sheets about many employees are available online and cover c1776 to the mid-1920s.

Births and Deaths at sea

On board ship records may also be a valuable resource particularly for deaths at sea or the occasional birth. To know who was on a particular ship we have a valuable collection of passenger lists not only for those generated in the late 1800s and throughout the 20th century but in periods beforehand where marine company archives may well contain details of both passengers and crew. In most instances looking at records in the destination country can be more revealing than those held in the originating country.

Any record made of a birth or death at sea from 1837 onwards was sent directly to the General Register Office and recorded in the Marine Register. No British merchant ship has ever been approved for marriages, (this includes passenger ships) although from 1854 any which took place had to be reported in the ship's log. Any marriages taking place on board a merchant ship was not legally valid, nor is there likely to be any certificate.

Child Migration

Many children were sent abroad under Government sponsored schemes and the records of the Childrens Overseas Reception Board, particularly the ships nominal rolls and Dept. of Agriculture reports, are an invaluable resource as these records show who the children were resident with in their destination country.

British child migration schemes operated from as early as 1618 to around 1967.

During this period, some 150,000 children were sent to the British colonies and dominions, mostly America, Australia, and Canada, but frequently also to Rhodesia and South Africa, New Zealand and the Caribbean. Many of these children were in the care of the voluntary organisations who arranged migration sometimes without parents being aware. The sole aim was usually to populate the colonies, to provide labour and increase productivity there.

Between 1869 and the early 1930s, over 100,000 children were sent to Canada. One of the first parties of young paupers to be taken to Canada was under the auspices of Maria Rye. Most of her migrants came from the schools for destitute children opened by Annie Macpherson in London and Liverpool in 1870, rather than workhouse schools. Such schemes had to arrange for the reception of the children in Canada and for their settlement.

Child migration is complex and involves research of the various government establishment records as well as the records of the care organisations or Board of Guardians. These resources should not be overlooked as part of the overall strategy in locating missing children.

There are some resources which may help locate details of individual children. Registers and case files of child emigrants can be found in the records relating to both Maria Rye and Annie Macpherson and to some extent the work of Dr Barnardo's can be found in the special collections archive at the University of Liverpool.

Canadian government inspectors' reports and statistical information regarding child migrants are in Parliamentary Papers.

In May 1940 because of the threat of invasion to Britain, Australia, New Zealand, South Africa, Canada and the USA took over 11,000 under private schemes which resulted in the creation of the Childrens Overseas Reception Board in June of 1940.

Around 3,000 children were sent to Australia, Canada, New Zealand and South Africa under the Reception Board scheme. There would have been many more had the evacuations not been stopped when SS City of Benares was torpedoed with the loss of 77 Canada-bound children. Many children returned to the UK after the hostilities to be reunited with their families. The records are held by the National Archives although many were destroyed along with other government records as a result of legislation passed in 1959.

Public Responsibility

Rates and Tax records

Everyone paid rates and taxes and these lists, where they survive, are, in effect, a census taken either annually or twice a year. Whilst they only cover heads of households they are at least proof of existence of a family at a certain time. They also provide vital clues as, when someone vanishes from a list, ask yourself what has happened, are they dead, have they moved? The answer is sometimes obvious if a widow or next of kin has taken over the responsibility.

Public Office

If your ancestor held a public office such as a magistrate, churchwarden overseer, surveyor or constable then there is a record of election primarily in Parish vestry minutes but verified by the Quarter Sessions. Often those offices generated a journal or ledger type record. Perhaps not full of detail about the individual ancestor, they can provide an insight into life and specifically show dates that someone was in the appropriate office.

Oaths of Allegiance

Another useful resource is oath rolls, particularly to show dissenting religious affiliations and also for those who held public office.

Between the 16th and 19th centuries various people, from magistrates, coroners and church ministers to merchants, lawyers, judges and members of the Royal Household and freemen of City livery companies, were required to swear oaths of loyalty to the Crown and the Church of England. In some cases, so did nonconformists. Most surviving oath rolls date from after 1673 and are available at the National Archives but some locally held Quarter Session records also include oaths or rolls.

Upon hard times

We have already addressed the situation regarding parish apprentices. When a family sought help and children within the family were of the right age, they were apprenticed with two outcomes in mind, firstly to reduce the financial burden on the poor rate and secondly and more long term, to help the family survive without needing poor law assistance.

Overseers records

Looking at the overseers' accounts and records will indicate when a family needed assistance. This could be a one-off payment for a coffin where a child has died, for medical help or just for subsistence. Such records may provide the vital clue to establish an event or situation. In many communities the need for assistance was on a regular basis so you will need to look at the whole volume to see the incidence of claims. (Such accounts, where they survive are part of the "parish chest" collections as are most of those discussed below).

Settlement and removal

One of the most valuable resources, particularly where a family has moved and you cannot easily find them, are the settlement and removal certificates which are all about parish of origin and movement around an area. These are loose documents and may not always survive but where they do the clue of a new or original location exists.

A settlement certificate was issued by the parish to which the family belonged, and the criteria of settlement could change throughout life. They were handed to the overseer of the destination parish. Therefore, there are two places in which a settlement certificate may be found. The original was kept by the issuing parish and the other copy by the destination parish. You will need to work out which parish records you have found the document in so that you do not mix up mobility. Some archives have name index lists of their holdings.

A removal order was issued when it was necessary for a family to be sent back to their parish of settlement. There was generally only one removal order and that would have been retained by the parish issuing the order in the first place.

Illegitimacy and bastardy records

Every family will encounter illegitimacy in one or more generations and to many this is the "end of a line". (Annoyingly this is obviously the continuation of the Paternal line as most records will continue showing only the mother's details). Looking for bastardy records is vital as these usually name the father because the mother is, in effect, suing for maintenance of the child. This clearly can open the door to tracing a paternal line but be aware as it is often the only proof you have of fatherhood.

Today a safer and sure way is to try and resolve the situation using DNA technology. – more about this later.

Militia Service

Throughout history the local Militia has been chosen by ballot where men of a certain age are listed and then when the militia is needed men from the list are chosen to perform the duties. When a man is away on Militia service his family are entitled to subsistence from the parish or militia authorities as the man is obviously not working. Militia Relief Orders usually held by the parish show the location of the man and the duration that he is away serving. They will generally mention family members resident at the time and can provide vital clues as to the numbers (or even names) of family members thus helping to determine the status of the family at the time.

Sometimes the Militia relief orders were sent to the militia pay office for re-imbursement so may be with Militia regiment papers rather than in the parish chest.

Workhouse and Poorhouse records

Since 1601 and particularly after 1834 families may have been admitted to the poorhouse or workhouse. Admission and Discharge registers for the "Union" workhouse provide information that may show the whereabouts of displaced family members. Most people were in the workhouse for one of three reasons, falling upon hard times, single woman about to give birth and as a means of receiving medical help or care usually in old age.

You will be able to find names of individuals and entire families listed in poor law records principally in the admission register along with the dates of admission, occupation, age, religion, parish and the cause of need for relief. Frequently a mother and her children are recorded together. Don't forget that for many families this was a way of life so they would be in and out with some frequency.

Poor law administrative records also contain information and correspondence relating to some inmates and will also include names and employment details of staff of the workhouse, Board of Guardian members and other employees.

The records most likely to be of help with family history research challenges relate to:

Births and/or baptisms that took place of workhouse inmates. If you cannot find a baptism in a parish or nonconformist register it may be because the child was baptised in the workhouse chapel. This is particularly true of illegitimate children. During the early period of civil registration, there are likely to be records of events recorded in these registers that would not show in the civil registration birth indexes. Workhouse registers give the name, birth date, and baptism date of the child, parents' names (or more likely the name of the mother), whether legitimate or illegitimate, and to what parish they belong or were admitted from.

Likewise, someone who died in the workhouse may be buried in a workhouse burial ground rather than being taken back to their parish or being interred in a municipal cemetery. These registers record both deaths and burial of workhouse inmates and include name, age, death date and again to what parish they belong. Be aware of age discrepancies which may happen because of uncertainty of age within the workhouse administration.

Admission and discharge registers are really the bible for research and record the name of the pauper, date of admission, age, occupation, religion, parish to which they are charged which would usually imply their parish of settlement, and the reason they required relief. When a pauper was discharged it gives the date of discharge, the parish to which charged, and how discharged. Many were discharged upon their own request. Remember these are chronological and depending upon how meticulous the record keeping system was will depend on whether you find someone admitted twice without discharge or vice-versa. Interpret what you find.

Creed registers which generally began in 1876 list name, date of birth, date and place of admission, religious denomination to which they attest, source of information i.e. who stated the religion, date of discharge or death. Some will also give occupation, last address and name and address of next of kin. They are a valuable resource for mobility and establishing a religious denomination at the time (which may of course change over time).

To some extent they mirror the admission and discharge registers but were often compiled periodically rather than daily so may show slight differences. I would not class these as primary sources but frequently they exist when admission and discharge registers don't. It is not always easy to trace inward and outward movements as very often a person is only entered once in the Creed register and that is generally when initially admitted. Discharge dates are very rarely recorded. In some unions the creed registers do record every admission and discharge.

The Indoor Relief List was also compiled from the admission and discharge registers twice a year. Sometimes the list was indexed and therefore could loosely provide a rough index to the corresponding admission and discharge registers. Indoor relief lists show if the pauper was able-bodied or not, whether an adult or child, occupation of pauper, when born, religion, and name. Sometimes all of this information is not always completed.

Outdoor Relief Books show the name of the pauper, when born, parish where residing, for how long relief was needed and amount of relief. Some only give the name of the pauper and a check-mark in a pre-printed column as to who they are and why they need relief. Outdoor relief was usually administered by the Parish Relieving Officer so there may well be more than one ledger for an area. Many such registers are by civil rather than religious parish so be aware of boundary differences.

The correspondence records are generally records of transactions between the Board of Guardians and the Poor Law Commission as well as details of local contracts for food, furnishings etc. These can include names of paupers and details of their grievance cases and the applications of persons wishing to be employed in the workhouse. Those generated from the Poor Law Commission are centrally held at the National Archives whilst those generated by the Board of Guardians are usually held locally. The Commission records are organized by union but are rarely indexed so can be difficult to use. Some are available online.

At any one time most workhouses needed a staff of around 50 people to function. The appointments of workhouse staff including masters, matrons, chaplains/clergy, medical staff, school teachers and porters are meticulously recorded. If you have ancestors who worked in the workhouse then the registers include full names, service dates, resignation or dismissal information, salary, and information on any allowances granted. The registers were only compiled from the 1840s and 1850s onwards, and so early and initial appointments are not usually shown but there are exceptions. You can also find CVs for workhouse staff and their appointment forms in the Poor Law Union correspondence. It can be frustrating sometimes because as staff left employment thick lines were drawn through the names making it sometimes difficult to interpret the information.

The Board of Guardians records include the minutes of their meetings. Staff notices of those leaving employment with the workhouse, including names, dates and reasons for leaving are also included in the Board of Guardians records.

Assisted Emigration

At the height of the Industrial revolution and for quite a period thereafter it was not unusual for families to be given the incentive to migrate to other areas of the United Kingdom or to pack up and emigrate being tempted with assisted passage and possibly even land grants in their new destination country. Many assisted passage schemes were administered by the poor law authorities and records of those emigrating can be found in vestry minutes (pre-1834) or records of the Boards of Guardians (post-1834). The British government had agreements with its colonies to make sure that new areas were populated. Many families would not have left other clues but just appeared to vanish. Researching these records may well open the door and provide an insight into your ancestors' family life at the time.

Land & Property Ownership

There are many records which will help in the location of an ancestor which are associated with land and property ownership. While most give only a "snapshot" view they can also be very revealing in detail.

Tithe Redemption

Both the maps and apportionments are very useful to identify the whereabouts of a family. Many family historians want to get an insight into where their ancestors worked and lived and this can help clear challenges. Created by the government, in a period from 1837 to the early 1850s, tithe records were the result of a very comprehensive survey into the usage, ownership and occupation of land in England and Wales. They relate to all levels of Victorian society and provide both names of the owners and the occupiers of land.

There are various search options. One set of documents would have been sent to the Parish to be kept safely, but in most cases the accompanying maps were too large to be preserved and may have been damaged, destroyed or exist in a poor condition.

A set went to the Church of England diocese in which the parish was located and can usually be seen at local record offices and another set of tithe apportionments and maps were sent to the Tithe Commissioners in London. It is these that are lodged with the National Archives. The tithe records are now available online.

Land Tax returns 1692 -1963

These provide a very good census substitute and supplement. It provides an annual list of proprietors and, in theory, the names of the actual occupiers in each parish. Because the list is annual, arrival and departure dates of an individual or family can sometimes be tracked by examining previous and subsequent land tax assessments. The four most northern English counties were taxed more lightly than many southern counties.

The returns can also become a good indication for inheritance and lead to clues about the death of an individual. The wealth status of an ancestor in comparison with their neighbours can sometimes be inferred from the tax list. However, there are limitations as not all the records have survived.

Names in the lists are usually male heads of households. There is also a risk of getting the wrong person. One common brick wall relates to a widow remarrying and as such property might be listed in the name of her second husband. Local assessments are not always straightforward to interpret. It is not always clear who were landowners and who were tenants or occupiers.

Some returns have been published are available online.

Returns of owners of land 1873-1875

The Return was produced from rate books by compiling and checking statistics already gathered on land and property ownership for the purposes of the Poor Law. They are a register of all landowners in England and Wales who owned more than one acre of land.

It was published commercially in 1875 and contains full name, address normally by location (town, village or area in town), amount of land owned and rental yields.

1910 Finance Act Valuation known as Lloyd George Domesday

These records were made for local tax administration following the 1910 Finance Act which provided for a valuation to be made of all property in the United Kingdom as at 30 April 1909. It resulted in the implementation of gross and rateable values which were used to assess the local rates paid by each householder.

The valuation process began during the summer of 1910 when landowners were sent a form which "an owner of land or any person receiving rent in respect of land" was required to complete and return to the district valuation office. The information extracted from these forms was entered into the valuer's field book and a physical inspection of all properties was made. The returns show the use of land and buildings and can be particularly useful for family historians. Maps were drawn up showing the location and extent of each property to be valued. This process took around five years to be fully completed and as such is a valuable companion to the 1911 census.

To find a property, you will need to locate the Ordnance Survey map sheet that was used as a way into the valuation field books. Each property is given a unique hereditament number, which corresponds to the survey entry in the field books. The country was divided into valuation districts and income tax parishes (nothing to do with either ecclesiastical or civil parish).

Once you've identified the right field book using that number you will see the valuation report for your ancestors' property. You will be able to find out the names of the owners, occupiers, extent of the land or property, its market and rateable value, dates of former sales, a brief description of the property and its condition. In some cases a sketch plan of the building and its outbuildings.

Personal and property deeds

These are a very neglected source of information, but like wills can provide concrete evidence of a family connection. Deeds include conveyances, marriage and family/personal settlements, leases, mortgage deeds, fines and recoveries. For the family historian they are the most abundant form of historical document, often unclassified (and thus not catalogued), dirty and ignored but they provide the crucial link in the sequence of family relationships.

Up to around 1735 deeds were often in Latin and could be difficult to read because of the legal jargon, but in many cases family history was included so there was no doubt about the title or inheritance. Permission for the sale of a property may be included, which may show a family tree and may have a baptism or marriage certificate lodged with it. They can also give clues to migration or even emigration.

In some areas they are easier to find than others. In 1708 an act of Parliament required registration of all deeds. In 1862 a National Land Registry was set up for voluntary registration. In 1899 a National Land Registry was introduced making registration compulsory.

The largest deed registries are those covering Middlesex and the Ridings of Yorkshire. Few other counties have registries. Researching requires a bit of thought and deeds may not always be easy to locate as they may be indexed by the unknown party but it is worth the effort in persevering.

Fire Insurance

Fire insurance offices were established in London from the late 17th century and in the rest of the country from the early 18th century. Almost all types of property, from domestic to industrial, could be insured, with the exception of property subject to fire risk or occupied by an unacceptable hazardous trade.

Policy registers are the main source of information. Where they exist they generally include the policy number, name, status, occupation and address of policy holder; names, occupations and addresses of tenants (where relevant); location, type, nature of construction and value of property insured; premium; renewal date; and any endorsements. These registers can be supplemented by claims records, surveyors plans and accounts. Often there are collections of actual policies and, in any case, it is always worth reviewing your family archive for such material.

Fire insurance maps are a valuable research tool alongside the policy registers. The plans drawn up by Charles E. Goad for business and retail property mainly in London from the mid-1880s include separate indexes covering street names, buildings and businesses and were regularly updated as fire insurance companies required accurate information.

Dealings with the law

Most of our ancestors would have had some involvement with the law. They did not have to be criminals or prisoners to appear in the records.

Criminal and prison records

Even if you are not aware of any proceedings it is always worth looking for records. Ancestors could be in court for petty crime, drunkenness, assault etc. so their misdemeanours may not have been known to any family members. Start with looking at local newspapers as they nearly always reported the proceedings of the courts no matter how minor the offence was. Remember that Petty Sessions and Quarter Sessions records are held locally while the Assize records are held nationally.

Similarly, prison records for county gaols are usually held locally but major prisons are again held nationally. You may even find a photograph of your ancestor because prison photography generally commenced much earlier than the family snapshot.

Remember also that those prisoners who ought to have been held in the national prisons were often housed in county gaols where the Prison Commission rented cells to use as overflows. The prisons involved were Aylesbury, Bath, Leeds, Leicester, Northampton, Nottingham, Preston, Reading and Wakefield.

Prison records are a valuable source of personal information as they usually included: age, marital status and number of children, whether they can read or write, trade or occupation, when and where convicted, crime, sentence, where and whence received, previous offences, when removed and where, birthplace, physical details, state of health and character in prison.

Ecclesiastical Courts

You will be surprised how many of our ancestors were involved in cases heard by the clergy. The most common were disputes over wills before 1858 but people appeared before the court for issues of marriage licences, non-payment of tithes, fornication and adultery as well as other moral misconduct of parishioners and legitimacy.

There may well be a cross over with secular civil courts and from the mid-19th century many ecclesiastical courts ceased to function in judgemental cases.

The ecclesiastical courts had the power to issue licenses for those wishing to work as apothecaries, midwives, surgeons and schoolmasters. Entries of such licences and petitions were written up in the court act books or sometimes in separate registers.

One thing to be aware of is that there was a court hierarchy and cases may have been heard in one of several courts, namely Archdeacons Court, Bishops (Consistory or Commissary) Court, Prerogative Court as well as in peculiar courts (if you ancestor resided in a Peculiar).

Records clearly relate to the functions undertaken by the church courts, including probate matters, marriage issues such as marriage licences, separation and legitimacy, licences for certain professions, church administration, recusancy (Roman Catholics) or non-attendance at church (nonconformists), church rates and tithes arrears. The courts also had jurisdiction on the 'moral' conduct of parishioners which usually revolved around sexual behaviour, drunkenness and similar vices. The courts also sat in judgement on matters involving their clergy and churchwardens as well as all matters concerning the day to day administration of the church. On occasions slander and libel cases were heard in a church court as well as or in place of civil court hearings.

Those of our ancestors who broke religious laws were normally presented to the court by the peoples' churchwarden. This process generated various records providing a wealth of information for the family historian. Presentments were presided over by the Bishop and were written up in books which listed the names of all the accused. These records form the main holdings for ecclesiastical courts and survive in large numbers. The court registrars recorded the events in act books which provided a summary of the case and sometimes a detailed account of proceedings. The citations, which summoned a defendant to court, contain useful details of the person and the person's parish.

From the mid 1600s the jurisdiction and authority of the courts declined as the powers of secular courts increased. By the mid-1800s civil courts had taken over virtually all the roles once dealt with by church courts particularly in the case of probate matters. However, up to 1858 church courts administered probate and dealt with cases of disputes so they may help resolve any associated challenges. Cases started just before12 January 1858 were usually completed in the ecclesiastical court they started in so it may be that for ten years or so after 1858 you would still need to refer to the ecclesiastical court records in cases of will disputes.

Ecclesiastical courts generally heard two types of case:

Office cases were brought to court by church officials and dealt with 'moral' and disciplinary matters such as bastardy, defamation and adultery, failure to attend Anglican services and other breaches of religious law. Cases were generally conducted orally so in many courts few records survive.

Instance cases were those taken to court by individuals and dealt with disputes such as defamation, tithe payments, marriage, probate and arguments over estates. Most written records of such cases include witness statements which are generally the most useful family history information. The deposition books were written in English. In an instance case, the process followed that which was usual in any court hearing where the plaintiff outlined the case against the defendant. Disputes over wills were usually heard as instance cases. However, it is sometimes difficult to establish if litigation actually took place. A disputed will case may have also been pursued through the Chancery or Exchequer court systems.

Defamation which was technically a crime could be heard as either type of case, depending on who the defendant was that was defamed. Most instance cases of defamation centred around accusations of sexual 'wrongdoing' including pre-marital sex, irregular marriages and adultery. Many women featured in defamation cases. If the court proceedings involved an illegitimate child then supporting Bastardy Documents will hopefully provide more information again opening up the Paternal line.

It is probable that new appointees would have signed an oath of loyalty and they may be recorded in Association Oath Rolls. The oaths originated and were organised in 1696 as a pledge of loyalty to William III. It was signed by all holders of public office such as MPs, freeman, military and civil officers of the crown, doctors, clergy and most people of some social standing.

The lack of transcription and indexing of the papers, the technical language, poor handwriting, irregular spelling, the heavily abbreviated style of writing as well as use of Latin before 1733 can be a slight impediment to research but the records are a valuable resource to resolve research challenges.

It is useful to understand the hierarchy of the church court system as many cases went to appeal or were dealt with by courts outside of the place of residence of your ancestor.

Archbishops' Courts – those of the Archbishops of York (PCY) and Canterbury (PCC) were known as 'Prerogative Courts'.

Bishops' Courts were either Consistory and Commissary Courts. These encompassed the bishop's diocese and were known as Consistories or, in the case of very large dioceses, the court's jurisdiction might be divided into smaller areas and were known as Commissary Courts.

Archdeacons or Archdeaconry Courts were below the Bishops' courts and were usually, but not always, the first local courts to deal with matters.

Certain parishes or groups of parishes usually independent of the local court of the archdeacon were known as 'Peculiar Courts' and were the sole jurisdiction for those areas.

Manorial Records

The manor was the principal administrative unit of landed estates from the medieval period up to 1925. Most ceased to formally function from the mid 1800s onward. Court business was carried out in the manor court before the steward. Manors varied in size but were administered by their Lords as a single unit. In the case of urban manors, records also contain details of markets, trade and industrial developments. Until 1733, many manorial records are likely to be in Latin.

Manorial records are classed as private records and for any manor may be held in different locations from being in private ownership or with solicitors (who may have succeeded as stewards' practices), to being deposited in either national and local records offices.

There were two kinds of manorial court: Court Baron and Court Leet with View of Frankpledge. Both court records need to be searched provided they exist.

The Court Baron was responsible for the internal regulation and affairs of the manor and was attended by all free tenants whose attendance at court was a condition of their tenure, and also by customary tenants. It was the principal type of manorial court which administered the customs (byelaws) of the manor and dealt with any offences against it. It also recorded the admission to and surrender of copyhold land making it a valuable resource for determining your ancestors' movement. It also dealt with various matters affecting the local community, such as the regulation of agricultural affairs and the enforcement of labour.

A Court Baron would typically have been held every three or four weeks in the larger manors, although for some manors the gap between court sittings could have been much larger perhaps only sitting twice a year.

The Court Leet was concerned with the enforcement of law and order. It received reports of the working of the frankpledge which was a "brother's keeper" system of mutual responsibility for the maintenance of law and order often referred to as the 'view of frankpledge'. It would also try minor criminal and civil offences such as assaults, obstruction of highways etc. It also dealt with the election of local manorial officials. The court leet normally sat twice a year.

Early manorial court rolls were normally written on parchment which were stitched together and made into rolls. From the mid sixteenth century it was not uncommon for the proceedings to be entered in a book volume. Each 'roll' began with the name of the manor and then the type of court, the name of the lord of the manor, where the court was held and when, and the name of the presiding official usually the steward. The business of the court was normally divided into distinct sections. There may well be a listing of the names of tenants who failed to attend the court; a record of changes in tenancy such as surrenders and admissions; a list of names of manorial jurors; a list of 'presentments', or offences to be considered by the jury; details of amercements, or fines, issued by the jury for offences; a list of 'pains', or regulations of the manor; and a record of the election of officials.

Accounts of the manorial income and expenditure would have been kept by the manor's steward or bailiff. Each account period began at Michaelmas (29 September) and took the form of a 'charge and discharge'. The 'charge' being the income from rents, the sale of produce or fines issued in the manorial court. The 'discharge' was a record of expenditure for such things as purchasing livestock, repairing buildings or paying for labour. Manorial accounts could be either a draft or final version.

Perhaps one of the most valuable documents to family historians is the rental which was a list of the names of all tenants who held land in the manor, together with a description of the land they held and a record of the rent they paid. Rents could be in cash or kind. Sometimes rentals might also include details of the services due from each tenant. Rentals were not made as frequently as court rolls or accounts and as a result, they may not survive in as large numbers. They would be organised in a fairly standardised way with the tenants listed by type of tenure, and then on a place-by-place or parish-by-parish basis.

Custumals were both the byelaws of the manor and a survey of rents, services and other obligations owed by tenants to the lord of the manor, and the rights and obligations of the lord. They formed a record of rights and obligations. The 'customs' would vary significantly from manor to manor.

Manorial records are often underused as they may appear daunting and off-putting to researchers because of the difficulties involved in locating and researching them.

Perhaps more significantly, though, there are the barriers of handwriting and language. Until 1733, manorial records were kept in Latin. The form of Latin was often very heavily contracted or abbreviated, and the type of handwriting used would vary from period to period.

Manorial records are not as inaccessible as they might first appear, however, as with deeds, they tended to be highly formulaic but adhered to a very standardised order and terminology. For finding the whereabouts of manorial records we have the Manorial Documents Register. This is available online for the majority of the country and is the key to location of records which may show they are held in several differing locations for the same manor.

To use the records effectively you will need some ability to read older forms of handwriting and to be familiar with standard formats and vocabularies of the manor but they will provide a surprising amount of information.

Manorial records are notable for being one of the few types of document where prolific information about ordinary people have survived from the medieval period.

For family historians and genealogists, manorial records are a useful resource, particularly for the period before extensive parish registers were kept. They are packed with lists of names, sometimes associated with details of occupations or of relationships. Sometimes they may include the age of an individual, frequently at the time of a surrender or admission, and they may include copies or extracts of wills, conveyances or mortgages. In this way, they can be invaluable in helping to build up rounded pictures of individuals.

One of the most interesting aspects of manorial records is the insight they give of the day-to-day life of ordinary people.

One aspect which is frequently overlooked when using manorial court records is the details about enfranchisement. This is where copyhold land was converted to freehold by the Lord. This was done by including an enfranchisement clause into a deed of conveyance, or by a separate deed of enfranchisement. Enfranchisement transferred the land from the Manor to an individual owner. The whole concept of enfranchisement was subject to complex legislation. Normally enfranchisements took place from the mid-1700s to around the early 20th century but tended to be more prolific from the mid-19th century. Some enfranchisement is still occurring today.

Enfranchisement is normally recognised by the beginning few words in a document which would state: "Hath granted bargained sold aliened released and enfranchised". The word 'enfranchised' will always appear. When copyhold tenure was abolished in 1922 and all remaining copyhold lands were turned into freehold, existing lords were able to claim compensation for the loss of revenue from their manors, (manorial incidents), and records are often found in the final court books of a manor or could be recorded separately within the stewards' papers.

Manorial records are most useful when not used in isolation but in conjunction with other records, including parish registers, enclosure maps and Quarter Sessions records.

Licences to Trade

Certain trades required the granting of a licence by the Quarter Sessions and it was often the case that ancestors moved around in practicing those particular trades. Trades for which a licence was most commonly required include gamekeepers, licenced victuallers and beer house keepers, badgers, hucksters and commercial travellers, butchers with slaughterhouses, and those operating printing presses.

On a slightly different tack certain societies also required Quarter Session approval such as Friendly Societies, Freemasons and Savings Banks, so again if your ancestor was involved at "officer" level with any of these then information may well be available to identify who, when and where.

There have been Acts of Parliament regulating the sale of alcoholic beverages since the 1552 Alehouse Act where recognisances (essentially character references) that the retailer would keep an orderly house had to be made before two justices. Clerks of the peace were ordered to keep an annual register of victuallers' recognizances in 1619, but few exist before the Licensing Act of 1753 made it mandatory. The registers can, and frequently do, contain the names of the licensees, the parish, the name of the inn (inn sign), the occupation of the victualler, and the names and occupations of those standing a surety bond. In 1828 the issuing of annual licenses commenced. Court sessions held solely for licensing of victuallers or pubs were called Brewster sessions and the records, where they exist for such sessions, can help trace an ancestor's location for a number of years.

Separation and Divorce

If your challenge revolves around a problematic marriage or you cannot find the death of a spouse when someone remarries then maybe they separated or divorced. The divorce process as we know it today commenced in 1858 but only case papers until the 1930s are accessible. It is one sure place to locate a marriage certificate if you have not been able to locate one in previous research. Divorce was fairly common after World War One but before then many people just separated usually by desertion (sometimes with mutual agreement). This of course gives rise to bigamy if either party remarried during the lifetime of the other, Bigamy was perhaps more common than we care to think – but try and prove it – that is a different thing!

If you suspect divorce or want to eliminate, then these records are for you. Before 1858 true divorce was by Act of Parliament and few people chose or could afford that route. However, separation was not infrequent and often the separation deed can be found in family papers or through a deeds registry.

Separation was often engineered particularly among the poorer community. People deserting from the workhouse very often went on to remarry or have second family sometimes within close proximity to their residence with a former spouse. The Poor Law Union Gazette, available online is a useful medium to confirm suspicion where a husband has deserted, leaving his family chargeable to the parish which was a criminal offence but was not always pursued.

Debtors and Bankrupts

You are unlikely to know if your ancestor was an insolvent debtor unless something gives rise to suspicious acts around the time. Prior to 1869 our ancestor as an insolvent debtor may well have been in debtor's prison for an undetermined period of time giving rise to all manner of situations. Most debtors were housed in the civil side of the local county gaol rather than in the traditional debtor's prisons. Sometimes local civil prison registers don't survive.

An insolvent debtor could remain in prison for an indeterminate period as the creditor frequently had the final decision on release via the Quarter Sessions courts, or if the debts remained uncleared. The evidence of an insolvent debtor or latterly a bankrupt could exist amongst Court statements, creditor affidavits and Bankruptcy Orders. Petitions for release from prison, usually found in Quarter Session records, where an imprisoned debtor could also petition a Justice of the Peace to be released. Look also at Prison Admission and Discharge records particularly where these are separate from criminal registers. Bankrupts, mainly traders or artisans, could pay the creditors even a proportion to discharge their debt. Insolvent Debtors who died in prison were also subject to a coroner's inquest so a search of local newspapers, or if you are lucky the coroners case records, is needed.

Bankruptcy is well documented through notices in the Government Gazettes and frequently in the local papers, particularly if your bankrupt ancestor was a trader or prominent local figure. You stand a chance of finding illuminating case records and financial statements although not all case records have survived. Bankruptcy records had to be kept for 25 years from the date of discharge after which they could be destroyed.

The Bankruptcy Commission Files at the National Archives also include Registers of Petitions for Protection from Process.

After 1832 the Court of Bankruptcy was established with creditors having to petition the Lord Chancellor and were then examined to determine the circumstances of the bankruptcy and set out a plan to recover the debts from the debtor. Once the Commission had established that the debtor was bankrupt a notice was published in the Gazettes. Once the bankrupt had discharged the debts a Certificate of Conformity was issued.

District bankruptcy courts were established after 1842 serving districts outside of London and after 1869 these district courts were merged with the County Courts. In London, the London Court of Bankruptcy, which was established in 1869, was incorporated into the High Court of Justice in 1884. Few district court records survive but where they do it becomes a valuable resource.

Information in Quarter Sessions Records

Quarter Session records started in the 13th century but for most counties and boroughs only exist from the 16th century onwards. These records dealt with the everyday events particularly as forerunners of local government. As the name suggests they were held four times a year. The court was open to all irrespective of social status. Among the records are:

Lists of names of justices of the peace, bailiffs, constables of hundreds, and jurymen, writs to the sheriff, to summon juries, officers, defendants and others, presentments, Indictments, bonds ensuring defendants and witnesses appear at the trial, lists of prisoners, usually stating the offence and often the sentence.

The records are also a valuable resource for matters of Settlement and Removal of Paupers and supplement the information likely to be found in the parish chest collections. Most examinations undertaken to determine settlement were recorded by the courts.

Quarter Session courts had magistrates and dispensed summary justice (i.e. without juries). Matters were sometimes referred to the higher courts to be heard before juries and be tried for indictable offences.

As we have seen by the 17th century many of the cases formerly heard in church court went to the Quarter Sessions. These included the huge amount of business generated under the Poor Laws and besides settlement and removal matters include vagrancy papers and poor apprenticeships, records of which may not survive in parish chests, bastardy orders and matters dealing with delinquent fathers and non-payment of tithes and taxes.

Until 1820 the Quarter Sessions dealt with about 200 different felonies.

Cases were frequently referred from local petty and borough sessions, where they existed, and the Quarter Sessions heard disputes and claims regarding everything from apprenticeships and soldiers' pensions to public nuisances. Many cases were routed to the new police courts during the 19th century, particularly in matters of bastardy. Quarter Session continued to sit as criminal courts for non-capital offences until 1971. However, capital offences such as murder and treason usually went to the Assizes, and divorce, probate, and shipwrecks at sea went to special courts.

Petty Sessions records and/or Justices Minute Books are the usual place to find a child support or maintenance order request known as an application of the mother after the birth of a bastard. Such cases were usually lodged within a year of the birth. It gives the name of the reputed father, his occupation and address, and may have been taken out even if the couple married just before the birth or afterwards.

If there were no petty sessions for the area try the quarter sessions. If an illegitimate child was residing in the workhouse then the Board of Guardians' relieving officer usually brought a case against the reputed father, as many fathers reneged on their maintenance payments. They were required until the child was 7 (and thus able to work!). By the 19th century the age was increased to 13. Bastardy complaints can be found up to the late 20th century.

Coroners' Inquests

The office of coroner began in 1194 and each originally had several responsi-bilities including confiscating the property of outlaws or more precisely those who had failed to show up in court, investigation of crimes, shipwrecks and treasure trove.

This was gradually restricted to the single duty of investigating the circum-stances of sudden, unnatural or suspicious deaths. The sole qualification until 1926 was that the coroner be a landholder. Since then a Coroner has to be a solicitor or qualified medical practitioner.

Coroners courts had a jury. The inquests were held at any suitable local building, often a local public house. The parish beadle or constable summoned witnesses who would include the local doctor, friends, neighbours and any relevant officials such as nurses or prison officers.

The record of the coroner's court lists the names of the jurors as well as the verdict. The coroner's bill usually included the name of the deceased, the date and place of inquest, cause of death and verdict.

Unfortunately, many coroners' records have been destroyed with most surviving ones from 1750 being at county record offices often within the Quarter Sessions records. Few modern coroners records survive. Local newspapers are usually more informative, giving significant detail of inquest proceedings from witness statements as well as final verdicts.

Death and after

Records of your ancestors did not cease at their death, in fact this group of records is perhaps the most valuable in locating information to overcome challenges.

Graves and memorials

I am assuming that in your quest for a missing ancestor that you will, as a matter of course, have explored wills and probate and also looked in obvious places for burials. However, what have you missed?

A popular Sunday afternoon jaunt amongst family historians is a visit to the graveyard. Some gravestones will be missing or impossible to read but many contain information which confirms their existence and death. Gravestones often act as memorials where people recorded on the stone are not actually buried in that cemetery or churchyard. Sometimes it is obvious, other times not so obvious. Remember also that information inscribed on the stone is only as good as that provided by the informant and may contain mis-information. (Many early gravestone transcripts exist having been undertaken before stones were removed or became unreadable because of weathering or vegetation growth or vandalism).

Some stones were erected long after the burial and often the clue is in the name of the mason (usually on the back of the monument). It may also reveal any known alias – more later.

You may also need to look at the local war memorial if trying to locate an ancestor who died during the First or Second World Wars and subsequent conflicts and was serving in the military or navy at death. Names were only included if the dependants paid or they were placed there by the community. Some families withheld names as a matter of principal. In my own village at least ten people who died in the First World War are not included on the war memorial for that very reason. It is recommended that looking for a memorial is fundamental to the search.

Cemetery Registers

Always look at the cemetery register and plan as well as a grave. Sometimes you need to do this first to locate the grave plot. Since 1854 municipal cemeteries have existed as alternative burial places to the churchyard. Again, they can provide valuable clues as many will also give the name of the undertaker and officiating minister. That minister can be from any denomination and is a big clue to religious affiliation of the family.

Looking at a cemetery register will also indicate who else is buried in the same grave which may be a relative whose details are, at the time, unknown.

In some instances, death may have occurred in a workhouse and if the family could not afford a decent burial the deceased would be interred in the workhouse graveyard where such existed, or maybe even sold by the workhouse for medical research in which case the only record will be that of the workhouse deaths and burials. If these registers exist and you cannot find a burial in the parish burials or cemetery register they are a good alternative.

Death memorial cards and post mortem photography

These are essentially family documents. It was very popular within families to circulate to family and friends a memorial card and from the advent of carte-viste photograph what is known as post mortem photographs. Nothing to do with an examination at death but purely a photograph of a family group or individual taken after their death. If they survive then they will inevitably be in a family archive or kept by family members as a keep-sake. The deceased was often photographed in age order with siblings and some photographers did a convincing job in making the deceased look "alive". You may have to look hard or know the hierarchy of the family to identify the deceased person in the photograph.

Undertakers records

Most funeral directors and undertakers will, from around the mid-1800s, have kept intricate records of the funerals at which they officiated. These are normally in the form of register books which detail such items as name, date of death and address of the deceased, what type of funeral service they had, where they were interred, who paid the funeral costs, the grave number, stonemasons instructions etc. They can be a valuable resource in identifying next of kin and also grave locations.

Many funeral directors will allow access to their records even if they have not been deposited with the local archives.

Because of the value of funerals, in the Victorian period particularly, you may also find receipts, funeral mementos and service programmes and items of mourning wear within a family archive.

In many provincial newspapers you will also find a potted history forming a person's obituary and perhaps details of the mourners together with their relationship to the deceased.

THE CLUE IS IN THE NAME

Without a name our research becomes tricky. What happens if the name is a common one and you cannot identify the right Smith or Jones or someone decides to call themselves by a different name? Think as well, how many people you know who are known by a name different to that which they were registered with, or even someone who is known only by their second forename, all of which can cause challenges.

The chances are that an ancestors' name change will be specific and happen at a certain time or for a certain reason. This may not be obvious to you at the time but will mean that you need to dig until you find the reason. Doing so may well be the key to successfully continuing your research and may reveal a legitimate reason for the change.

A possible change of name ….

1. Should automatically ring bells
2. Allow you to suspect a possible skeleton – crime, bigamy, under-age army enlistment, persecution etc.

However, anyone can change their name at any time during their lives without recourse to legal documentation. In fact few people actually used the legal process to change a name. Let us therefore look at some of the possible difficulties that can be found around name sources.

Simple spelling variations

Before standardised spelling of surnames scribes wrote down what they heard, and thus a surname (or forename) will be spelt phonetically. Because many of our ancestors could have been illiterate they had no idea, if they even saw the record, whether their name was spelt correctly or not (if indeed it could ever be determined what the correct spelling of the name was).

Finding a person can become problematic if searching alphabetical listings particularly if you maintain a narrow approach thinking that a surname could only ever be spelt the way you spell it today.

In my own family history, I have at least two lines which illustrate the point.

On my paternal line I have the Albone family. I have found the name spelt in the following ways (this is not comprehensive) Alban, Owlborn, Auburn, Holbourn, Holbon, Holbone, Awlburn, Albon.

On my maternal line I have the name Shouler spelt in the following ways but this time the first letter has not changed but is equally phonetic. Shewler, Shoulder, Showler, Soueller, Sheweller, Shoveler.

Shouler is not so much a challenge as Albone but nevertheless can present a few challenges to the inexperienced. I would venture to suggest that most people will

80

find their name spelt in a variety of ways so just be open minded in your approach. This is particularly significant when looking at alphabetical listings such as civil registration, probate calendars etc. Apparently, there are thirty-two ways to spell Smith!

Those of you who have reached the period before parish registers will encounter other challenges with surnames. Besides the large number of spelling variations, you will be fringing on Latin or Anglo-Norman. Surnames only became hereditary for all levels of society in the early 14th century. Prior to that persons were described in more than one way e.g. Robert Lascome of Northampton could also be Robert Northampton, Robert of Northampton, Robert le Mercer of Northampton etc.

 Ignore name spelling variations at your peril. Remember that before standardised spelling names were recorded as heard by people. It only needed a slightly deaf official listening to a name stated by your ancestor who spoke with a dialect or accent and a wonderful array of spelling variations would be written down.

Traditional naming patterns

In family history we normally place our emphasis on surnames as they are usually the only way of identifying generational families. Surnames are generally inherited and although they can change, some form of it is usually retained. Forenames are equally important. They individually identify a child based upon the choice of the parent or on a traditional naming pattern which is usually generational or the subject of local tradition.

You will frequently see the same names used over and over again in families. This is not due to narrow-mindedness or lack of imagination on the part of the family. It can represent a possible religious following or just be a popular name in the area or in different times in history. Christian names are subject to fashion and are often shaped by events or the popularity of a famous person at the time. Many cultures believe in honouring their elders and do so by naming children after them. One of the most common but my no means elite patterns is that used over a period spanning c1700-1875:

> The first son was named after the father's father
> The second son was named after the mother's father
> The third son was named after the father
> The fourth son was named after the father's eldest brother
>
> The first daughter was named after the mother's mother
> The second daughter was named after the father's mother
> The third daughter was named after the mother
> The fourth daughter was named after the mother's eldest sister.

If this pattern resulted in a duplication of names where, for example, both grandfathers had the same name then they would skip to the next one on the list or add a second forename so one child would be William and the next John William and be known a Johnny etc. I would however warn against giving naming patterns too much credence as it would be very difficult to follow exactly. As a finding aid it is usually a good guide.

You may also see names of parents and grandparents, siblings, aunts and uncles repeated but not in any order. It is sometimes difficult to establish who William or John or Ann or Mary was actually named after. While many names in a family will probably appear to be repeats, there will always be totally different ones which are unusual or unique to that family group. A child might be named after a friend or a popular personality of the time.

Even if the family did not follow a naming pattern, the repetition of names can be significant, especially where they have used an unusual name. Many families chose to use religious names and when these children married, they tended to use the same names for their offspring. There may even be a naming pattern established in this regard.

Some families may exhibit a liking for one name.

Up until the 20th century families experienced high rates of infant mortality so if a child died, the name was often used again for the next child born of the same gender.

Always note carefully a surname (or a name that sounds like a surname) that is given as a second forename. Very often the same second forename is given to more than one child. Although not hard and fast the maternal side will often be revealed through the use of family surnames used as forenames for children.

Nicknames

Nicknames that existed in Victorian times and earlier especially for females, may be unfamiliar to you because they are not in common use today. The examples given below may or may not be familiar.

> Margaret: Maggie, Rita, Madge, Greta, Peggy, even Daisy
> (Marguerite is the French word for Daisy)
> Mary: Polly, Minnie, Polette
> Minerva: Minnie
> Alice: Lisa, Sonny
> Amelia: Milly
> Helen: Ailene, Elaine, Leonora, Nelly
> Sarah: Sadie
> Louise: Alison, Eloise, Lois

Male nicknames are usually more straightforward, although some are not quite as obvious as others. It was more common for men to use their second forename than have a nickname for common use, thus everyone will know them by their middle name. A slightly different approach is if you have, for example, a John William. He could be known as Bill throughout his life. You may however search for example a census looking for Bill or Wm. and find he is recorded just as John. Male nicknames are generally more obvious.

Cornelius: Neil, Cory
William: Bill, Billy, Will, Willy
John: Jack, Ian, Iain, Johnny
Henry: Harry, Hal
Albert: Bertie, Al, Alb, Alby

Some nicknames have more than one association in their origin e.g. Rich for Richard, Frederick, Eric.

During the 1800s it was also fashionable for children to be named after a prominent person of the time be it a member of the Royal family or perhaps a well-known music hall star or prominent scientist. Fashionable names are generally "short-lived" but can become traditional with a family if the name was liked.

 Nicknames were commonly used during the lives of our ancestors so it was not unusual for people to appear on census records and other documents with the pet name or nickname or even with a prominent second forename. Subsequent records of an individual may not record their official registered birth name.

Name Changes recorded on gravestones

Very often a name change, or more importantly an alias, is shown on monumental inscriptions. It is always necessary to visit the cemetery or graveyard where your ancestor is buried and record the information on a gravestone. Where a gravestone has been removed look to see if an early monumental inscription for the churchyard or cemetery was taken before the removal.

Statutory declaration

Very often there are additional notes and alterations made on certificates of birth, marriage or death. These were added when something had been omitted or when a mistake had been made at the original registration. This was normally done after the date of the event and is frequently the subject of a statutory declaration or endorsment by the Registrar General. If necessary purchase certificates as the information may be a valuable source of detail in resolving a challenge.

Sometimes if you have located a marriage certificate then there may be additional information included in a parish register entry and vice-versa. I am not suggesting that it is necessary to obtain every certificate for every post 1837 marriage but all too frequently information can be different so, if you suspect something is amiss then searching "every available source" is needed.

Name changes

There are a variety of reasons why someone changed their name. The following are just some examples:

Some immigrants changed their name as part of the naturalisation process. In 1916 enemy aliens in Britain were forbidden to change their names and this process was extended in 1919 to all foreigners and the restriction was not abolished until 1971.

Foreigners frequently anglicised their surnames to fit in with society and this was particularly true of artisans and the business community or those desiring to serve in a public office. As a proportion, the number of foreigners who became British citizens through the Naturalisation process was minimal. Beware of the census entry which states "naturalised British citizen" it can be misleading and as such no naturalisation papers can be located. It was terminology used by enumerators often incorrectly interpreted.

Those who fled to Britain because of political or religious persecution had a desire to conceal racial origin and to avoid detection by their own country's officials.

Illegitimate children often changed their names and would often adopt the surname of their mothers' husband after her subsequent marriage even if that person was not their natural father.

In certain circumstances a child would be brought up as a child of grandparents sometimes taking a surname of the grandparent which could be different from a birth name depending on which set of grandparents reared the child.

As a matter of course, any child who was in the care of the Foundling Hospital, and that was something like 250,000 throughout its existence, would be renamed and baptised in their new name virtually upon admission. Baptism registers will not give any clues about the original name.

The Foundling Hospital had several satellite establishments throughout the country at Aylesbury, Westerham, Chester, Shrewsbury, Barnet and Ackworth. Whilst most information is held collectively there may well be some information in the record offices covering the satellite areas. Former school pupils and their relatives can obtain access to the papers relating to themselves on application to the Coram organisation. To research further you need to identify, from a variety of sources, the number given to the child on admission. The records of the Foundling Hospital are held by the London Metropolitan Archives.

Anglicised Irish surnames

There were various ways in which the Irish anglicised their surnames and this can be confusing when the time comes to revert to Irish records to further your family history.

The most common way was by phonetic spelling when the surname was written as it was pronounced without regard to the way it was spelt in Ireland such as O'Brien for O'Briain or O'Callaghan for O' Ceallachain. The Irish name could also be subject to dialect variation thus giving rise to different spellings in different parts of the country. In many cases an Irish surname would have been contracted and not infrequently, only part of the original form would have been retained. The most common contraction is by the dropping of the O' or even further where for example the name Ryan was originally O'Mulryan.

Throughout the 19th century and early 20th century particularly after the mass migration as a result of the potato famine, families frequently rejected phonetic surnames in favour of adopting an "English" style of surname. This became accepted as the English translation of the Irish surname. Add to this the confusion that can arise because some Irish families had and used two surnames each taken from a different ancestor.

If you have Irish ancestry you will need to be aware of the Irish naming patterns prevalent at the time your ancestor lived and these can vary from area to area of Ireland.

Welsh patronymics

The tendency to anglicise Welsh names can also present a hurdle for genealogists. Patronymics is giving a child the father's given, or forename, as a surname. This means that a family's name changes in successive generations and sometimes with each child of the family. Patronymics are complex.

For example, Rhys ap Dafydd translates as 'Rhys, son of David'. Modern Welsh surnames such as Powell, patronymically would have been ap (meaning son of) Hywel and are the result of this contraction and a progressive tendency to Anglicise Welsh names. ap in Welsh means son of and ab means daughter of.

The process of converting to the system of fixed surnames in Wales began as early as the fifteenth century and continued through to the start of civil registration in 1837.

Before 1837 the official recording of births, marriages and deaths further complicates the issue. The1536 Act of Union stated that all official documentation in Wales was to be carried out in the English language. This meant that Welsh names were registered in an anglicised form. Civil registration completed the transition to fixed surnames. In many parish records, and particularly in nonconformist registers the use of patronymics continued thereafter, suggesting a person may have had two names!

It is important in Welsh research to remember the existence of Patronymics. It may be that your family dropped Patronymics a long way back so it may not affect you, but it's wise to be aware of the process. Patronymics didn't cease at the same time in all areas of Wales and began to die out in some areas much earlier than others.

In England, names ending with the suffix "son" were often originally patronymic and the use of "Mac" in its various forms, was prevalent in Scotland, Ireland and the Isle of Man used also to denote son of ......

Military and Criminal Alias Names

It was fairly common for alias names to be used for both military service and criminal activity. The reasons for the latter may well be obvious but for military service perhaps not quite as clear.

Military alias's, although used throughout history, were more prevalent in enlistments which preceded the First World War. This was particularly true amongst the early volunteers when there was a rush to serve, particularly in the army. Many Pals Battalion enlistments include alias names. In many instances the alias name is written on the attestation form but there are other elements which can cause confusion.

Many people with German sounding names used alias names or just literally anglicised their name, some of which were not obvious. It is then difficult to identify an ancestor unless some prior knowledge of the alias name is known. For those who survived the war those surnames tended to be used in later generations but if your ancestor was killed it is unlikely that the name will be known unless the family adopted the name.

Those who wanted to enlist under age very often did so using a friend's name or even an older brother's name to try and avoid parental interference or objection. Technically this was not an alias but deliberate misuse of a name. This becomes quite confusing if the older brother also enlisted using his own name. It is often necessary to employ good detective skills to distinguish as it is unlikely that the person whose name was used was aware of the deceit. Parental objection very often meant that the child ran away to enlist under an alias before parents realised what had happened. If the parents wanted to object or went to the authorities there would effectively be no record of the person enlisting!

Some people used an alias name to avoid detection where a past military career existed and they had at some time deserted or been the subject of a court martial. Because of the keenness to enlist for the Great War they chose again not to be traceable in military records.

For criminals the interesting thing is that most records will show one or more alias names but it does not follow that all the alias's will have been discovered. For the habitual criminal, intelligence usually identifies all the names for the record and many criminals confessed to other crimes divulging the alias names to soften the sentence when taken through the courts.

There are also "gender bender" alias's where male names were used by females and vice-versa. A classic and fairly well-known example is that of Harry Crawford, alias Eugenia Falleni whose crime in 1920 was murder. Harry spent most of his life masquerading as a woman and he was even flouting marriage laws. Crawford or rather Eugenia, as appeared on the marriage certificate, married widow Annie Birkett who he later murdered. Maybe this was the first "same sex marriage" of the 20th century!

Change of name by Deed Poll

A deed poll is a legal contract relating to one person and is essentially a private document which may only come to light in family archives. It was sometimes recorded in the enrolment books of the Supreme Court (formerly Chancery Close Rolls). Not all deed polls were registered.

If people desired to make name change more official, they usually made announcements in the press and sometimes made a declaration before a Justice of the Peace or Commissioner for Oaths drawn up as a "deed poll".

The earliest date for finding a deed poll is c1851 using Chancery records. Indexes and the enrolment books for 1903 to 2003 are at the National Archives in class J18. The indexes show both the former and the new name, either as a note or a cross-reference.

 There may never be an official record of a name change, but usually it occurred with a clean break from the original name and it is worth trying to find a reason that someone did change their name.

Enemy Aliens

In 1916, enemy aliens resident in Britain were forbidden to change their names and in 1919 this was extended to all foreigners living in Britain. This ban was not lifted until 1971.

There were several exceptions, namely: if a new name was assumed by royal licence, if special permission was given by the Home Secretary or if a woman took her husband's name ar marriage.

In all cases it would be advisable to search the London Gazette in the first instance and follow through on any clues.

Royal Licences

Royal licences to a change of name were common in the 18th and 19th centuries, but in later years would be issued where: an inheritance depended on someone taking the deceased's name, a marriage settlement required a husband to adopt his wife's name or a change of name also required a change to a coat of arms. Information about Royal Licences is held in various places including the National Archives and the College of Arms. Notices again appear in the Gazettes.

Name change by Act of Parliament

Some changes made were by Act of Parliament although there have not been any since 1907. The reason that someone would want a change by an Act are basically the same as those reasons shown for Royal Licences. Records can be accessed by the Parliamentary Archives but it is advisable to use the Chronological Table of Private and Personal Acts (1539-2006) to locate an Act before pursuing the case research.

Phillimore and Fry Index to name changes 1760-1901

The Index to Changes of Name for UK and Ireland is an extremely useful reference to name changes and is taken from the following sources of information:

1. Private Acts of Parliament
2. Royal Licences published in the London and Dublin Gazettes
3. Notices of changes of name published in The Times after 1861 with a few notices from other newspapers
4. Registers of the Lord Lyon [King of Arms] where Scottish changes of name were commonly recorded
5. Records in the office of the Ulster King at Arms
6. Some private information

It does not include changes by Royal Licence which were not advertised in the London Gazette or changes by deed poll that were enrolled but not advertised in The Times newspaper.

Clean Break or Mystery?

For the genealogist or family historian, going back and finding someone has changed their family surname can be extremely frustrating. In many cases the break between old and new surnames is a clean one, so it can prove very difficult, if not impossible, to find the original name, leaving you with a dead end that can prove impossible to resolve.

Even if you can, you might never discover exactly why that ancestor chose to make a change, - just adding to the mystery.

CAN'T READ THE HANDWRITING

The more you research your family history the more you will be able to read the handwriting of the various documents. Even 20th century handwriting can be problematic but if you cannot interpret a name or other vital information in a document you will end up either not being able to solve your challenge or ignoring a document which is really of interest to you.

In most documents there are two aspects which usually present a challenge, namely:

Names

Capital and confusing letters

Capital letters do not stand alone but need to be treated alone otherwise you may be guessing at what they say. They are often preceded by a flourish which can confuse. Take the letter "H" for example.

Handwriting styles

Not only does the style of handwriting change over time it is also affected by other factors.

DEPARTMENTAL STYLE – the courts and government departments had their preferred styles which was used by clerks and other officials who could write in that style.

SCHOLASTIC TEACHING – Different types of schools taught different styles, Grammar and Public were different to National Board and ecclesiastical / monastic schools.

SCRIVENERS COMPANY – had a unique style to show that the scribes were members.

Most scribes were either of the legal or religious professions and most learnt their writing style at school. Generally, the further back in history the document originated the more precise the style of writing. Although there was a set style, individuals all wrote in a unique way.

Handwriting styles vary over the different periods of history with the main styles being Chancery, Court Hand, Secretary Hand and Italic Hand, the latter perhaps being the nearest in style to "modern" handwriting although originating much earlier.

Secretary hand:

Chancery Hand:

Italic Hand:

Legal Hand:

Cursive Hand:

Mixed Hand:

Guidelines for reading old handwriting

Read through the whole document even if you do not understand it. Extract the words you are able to read. If you have a photocopy of the document highlight the words which are unclear. To recognise more difficult letters and words compare them with the words you can read. Sometimes it is necessary to consider the context rather than spelling out the word. Don't guess.

Build up your own alphabet of capital and lowercase letters. (You will be surprised how many letters can be obtain from words like and, but, to, item, when, etc. all of which are usually fairly easy to read).

Once you are ready to transcribe your document then you need to NUMBER the lines and on your copy number each line at each side of the script. It is very easy to drop down a line or miss something if the lines are a little close together or have elevated script and having a number at both ends tends to avoid this happening.

Transcribe line by line writing out the text EXACTLY as it is written (do not try to put it in modern English)

Miss out any word you cannot read and then go back and fill the word in letter by letter. (The word may repeat itself more clearly later in the document).

Try and establish what any abbreviations or contractions mean which exist in the document.

Practice is essential – the more you read old handwriting the more familiar you become with styles, the easier it is to read. Likewise become familiar with the terminology of various documents. Many words are no longer used and items like coffers and bolsters, whilst common in the Victorian period, are not used today. Many unusual words exist in wills and inventories which are, of course, valuable family history documents. If you don't understand what the words mean or represent you are at a disadvantage from the beginning.

Some examples:

YELDING – brewing

TOFT – messuage or homestead

LANDIRON – gate to field

PALLIAS – straw or horse-hair mattress

COFFER – lockable box or chest

COD – pillow or cushion (often as lacemaking)

BARROW – boar or pig

Familiarity with both the writing and terminology used will make transcription easier. An incorrect transcription can completely change the meaning or make something relate to someone it shouldn't.

Names can be challenging – look at the following examples for William:

There are other challenges associated with reading writing in the form of punctuation, line fillers and contractions or abbreviations, all of which varied with different styles and time periods.

Incomplete Words

Contractions - The omission of one or more letters in the middle of a word

comon	Common
conditon	Condition
remebrance	Remembrance
ꝑ ꝓ ꝑ ꝑ	per par pre
pish	Parish
pfect psents.	perfect presents

Superior letters - Raising of some letters above the line (some may also be omitted)

w^t	with
w^ch	which
ye y^t	the that (using Y as THORN)
Jno	John
Matie	Majesty
testa^t	testament
ten^t	tenament

92

Suspensions - End few letters of a word omitted (abbreviations).

Difficult and confusing letters

If you try and relate lettering to modern styles then you will come unstuck when interpreting what a document says. There are several confusing letters such as c, e, r and s.

In early alphabets there was no letter J.

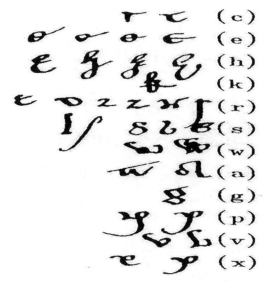

Why are lower case letters difficult?

Many are often joined at the top instead of the bottom as in modern styles.

The letters c, e and r are particularly confusing as they may all look the same.

An s can look like an f if the long form is used. Where ss is used in a word it can also be fs or sf or ff.

The letters i, m, n, u, v & w can be confusing where used as minims as in "community"

Punctuation:

/ Forward slash was used instead of a full stop – known as a VIRGULE

" ( ) Inverted commas were not used as we use them today. These and brackets were fully interchangeable

' Apostrophes were generally not used. If they were they denoted a plural rather than a missing letter.

= Equals signs were generally used as we would use hyphens today.

Various marks (usually curls or waves) were used at the end of lines as space fillers particularly in legal documents. Often confused with minims

Numbers

In some instances, numbers can be as confusing as letters. Clearly numbers are important for dates, ages etc. so a clear understanding is needed.

1 ꝑ ... (handwritten forms of the number one)

2 ... (handwritten forms of the number two)

3 ... (handwritten forms of the number three)

4 ... (handwritten forms of the number four)

5 ... (handwritten forms of the number five)

6 ... (handwritten forms of the number six)

7 ... (handwritten forms of the number seven)

8 ... (handwritten forms of the number eight)

9 ... (handwritten forms of the number nine)

10 ... (handwritten forms of the number ten)

It is easy to mix up some numbers with letters so beware. The numbers 2, 7 and 9 can be particularly confusing as can be seen from the list above. Obviously, misinterpreting dates can lead to further research challenges.

 There is only one way to become proficient in reading old documents and that is by experience. The more you read documents the easier it will be to understand forms and styles. Initially it would benefit you to take a course in palaeography. There are several online courses which are available at no cost. If you are not sure of what a document is telling you ask someone who has experience.

WAYS TO OVERCOME THE CHALLENGES OF RESEARCH

The single-minded approach

There are several keys to mitigating the challenges of any research and some of us just find it difficult to achieve these because of our enthusiasm for the research.

Stay Focused
Plan your research
Don't get side-tracked
Understand your family history
Be persistent – this also involves patience

Don't give up if you don't find anything. A negative search is as positive as a positive search because you can eliminate. However, maybe you need to review your plan or look again at your family history. You have probably missed something or are in the wrong place.

 If you find you are getting negative search results then the chances are you are looking in the wrong place. Review your research and think about your research strategy. You are probably looking at the wrong records or in the wrong locality.

What the records don't tell us

The full picture can never be gained from one document because each document exists for a different purpose (usually nothing to do with tracing family history). I re-iterate the fact that you need to know why a record was originally created.

It is also necessary to look at a variety of records to obtain all the clues.

Everything you want, irrespective of location, will not be held in one single record office.

Another pair of eyes!

If you are stuck on an aspect of your research that has become a challenge ask someone else to look at your research to analyse what you have found. Sometimes even those who have no knowledge of family history can pick up the obvious that you have missed. Remember no one except you wants to be subject to long missives about your family! Discuss your logic and thinking with them and pick their brains. Most people in the family history community are happy to help and may have encountered similar challenges. They may pick up an obvious omission or confirm what you think. They could also suggest trying a different avenue.

Read Q & A sections of family history magazines as well as the articles. Most of these relate to research challenges and brick walls encountered by fellow enthusiasts. Many interesting scenarios and situations are sent into the editors of the family history press who use professional genealogists or subject experts to try and put you on the right track. There are often useful hints, ideas and processes recorded in the answer/responses to questions.

Hashtags, Tweets and Blogs

Today social media plays a great part in family history and can be equally effective in helping to resolve research challenges. It is the new language of family history but requires caution as information could easily be false or misleading. However, it is another avenue to work in trying to resolve your challenge.

When I first started researching in the 1970s, the Internet was in its infancy and there were no social media sites such as Facebook and Twitter. Contacting people who were researching your family would usually be by your family history society members interest page and sending a member a letter.

I appreciate the potential intrusiveness of social media sites, and indeed this has put me off being heavily involved in this activity. If you use it wisely, then social media can provide you with huge benefits.

The two most popular sites for contacting the family history community have to be Facebook and Twitter but there are many others that can be effectively used such as Instagram, Pinterest, Google+ and even You Tube.

These sites offer you the chance to meet new family members. You might initially feel uncomfortable using these platforms but once you have the confidence they can help you reach a new audience and expand your family tree.

The most obvious benefit to using social media is that you will potentially find people researching the same family line as you and this enables you to meet family you did not know you had and enables you to collaborate your research efforts.

You will need to be careful with the information you share initially until you have established a definite family connection. Once established, it can be a great advantage to pool ideas and share experiences, photographs of the family and maybe arrange to meet up.

 Social media is not without its issues when it comes to sharing family history. Not every claim is accurate and users may use a profile unconnected picture or, for whatever reason, may say they are from a place to which they have never been.

Facebook

Facebook lends itself to creating a family page or group or connecting with genealogical societies, organizations, and specialist groups. By doing so you can find and connect with distant cousins or family members in foreign countries. Learning from peers is one of the easiest options that may not have occurred to you so why not join or create a Facebook genealogy group. If you are already a Facebook user you can easily create a group and open the door to collaborating on many aspects of genealogy.

If you find a document difficult to read or you have documents in a foreign language or Latin you could try one of the genealogy translation groups as it is quite likely someone will be able to help. There are also resources for many religious denominations so if you have nonconformists there may be specialist help available such as with Jewish genealogy.

Many existing and well-established groups have their own rules about what you can and cannot post, and which details you need to provide so that people can help. If you are creating your own group then you need to establish your rules at the outset.

For a so-called "brick wall" in your research then these groups can be invaluable. Maybe you have exhausted all your ideas and want to know if you overlooked something. If you want to try and find other descendants in your family then asking in a Facebook genealogy group could help you come up with a fresh approach or make you aware of new resources to try.

As with any internet interactions such as blogs, speciality groups, social media sites etc. you will need to observe any codes of conduct and also not give away personal information which will remain in the public domain forever. For this purpose, it is usual to have an administrator/moderator to control content and responses.

The following are basic etiquette tips for posting and commenting in Facebook genealogy groups:

Read the rules of the group before posting.

Do as much work as you can on your own first.

Include as many details as possible for your ancestor but be very cautious about including information about yourself.

Don't advertise any services or businesses within the group.

Reciprocate with help where you can. People will be more likely to help you in return.

Twitter

Twitter is used in a slightly different way but is a good way to find people with common surname interests. Posting on twitter and using the hashtag facility is a pretty good way of reaching people that are not your followers but who share a common interest in a subject or name that you have tweeted about.

To use a hashtag (#) on Twitter you add words after the tag. As people search Twitter against that hashtag their search will bring up all of the Tweets that used the hashtag. In this way one single hashtag tweet could connect with those who are interested in the subject making it easy to share information on Twitter.

If you have a research challenge (or even if you just want to contact people) consider setting up a family hashtag name to promote your own family name. You can obviously follow all the well-known genealogy sites on twitter such as archives, libraries, magazines, and family history organisations, which will potentially keep you fully up to date with all the latest family history news.

Twitter # Ancestry Hour

This is a Twitter base for everyone in the family history world where you can meet, exchange tips, ask questions and engage with international family historians. It operates every Tuesday evening between 7pm and 8pm GMT or 8pm and 9pm in British Summer time. It also has a dedicated website running blogs, newsletters etc. https://www.ancestryhour.co.uk/

The Family History Community

Users of the internet will be aware of the additional resources that are around to help you in your quest.

Forums

    Blogs

    Groups

    Message Boards - such as "curious fox" where you can request help in identifying a family name or a place

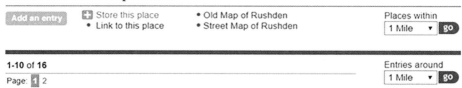

Rushden Northamptonshire

Add an entry	➕ Store this place • Link to this place	• Old Map of Rushden • Street Map of Rushden	Places within 1 Mile ▾ go

1-10 of 16

Page: **1** 2

Entries around
1 Mile ▾ go

✉ **Bletso/e**
We are looking for anyone with a Bletso/e family member to contact us please. No matter where you are in the world. If you have any family stories or pictures we would love to hear all about them. This is not a one name study but a family trying to get to finding long lost relatives. Look forward to hearing from you. D & C

✉ **Litchfield, Hooton, Rushden, Northamptonshire**
Looking for any relatives or information on the Litchfield or Hooton Families of Rushden.

✉ **Bayes families, Rushden**
Seeking information on Bayes families in the Rushden area, particularly Ernest Bayes, killed in India in 1944. Three sons were then sent to orphanages at Raunds and Bisley. the family lived in Pemberton Street, rushden, it is believed.

✉ **Bazeley Harry George died 1968**
Lived King Street buried town cemetery Rushden -employed sometime in boot& shoe trade father of Mabel Stapleton& Dorothy Litchfield. Any help tracing family ancestors/ descendants welcomed for our family history enquiries.

✉ **Britton/Brittaine family**
Looking for any information regarding the Britton/Brittaine family and in particular Thomas Britton born in 1644 in Higham Ferrers/Rushden.

✉ **Richard Higgins**
I am looking for Richard Higgins he was living in Rushden 1851 and married Sarah ?? they had 6 Children He had a farm in Woollon in Water Lane does anyone have any info??

✉ **Rushden Northamptonshire**
I am looking for information about John Bletsoe born c 1724. He married Mary Darling from Rushden but I cannot find his baptism there. He may have been born in Wellingborough, the son of John a Tanner. Can anyone help?

Podcasts - offering free video instruction from organisations like FamilySearch or the National Archives.

Family Trees - but beware of those which appear on many commercial sites, remember that information is frequently false or totally inaccurate but there is a remote possibility that they may provide clues and finding aids for you to pursue.

Wikis – Free ideas and information about documents, handwriting etc.

Website Blogs – usually specific to the subject of the website and frequently very informative and up to date.

Family History Societies – Most family history societies have their own website with much information and datasets relating to their own county or area of speciality.

Consider DNA testing

This book is not intended as a guide to DNA nor to investigate the pros and cons of the subject but merely to offer this suggestion as an additional resource to help overcome research challenges.

DNA testing is an increasingly important tool to help to verify your family tree and provide helpful clues to enable how you plan the future direction of your research. It can also sometimes help to break down those long-standing research challenges and brick walls. DNA is now an essential tool for the family historian and not just for those with challenges. It can be used to confirm theories about relationships and can provide answers that can't be found using the paper trail despite the variety of records we generate in our lives. Not all DNA testing facilities are going to provide you with accurate, reliable or thorough information. There are many DNA testing scams also and to avoid scams and low-quality testing labs, make sure you seek a testing provider that has some form of accreditation in the family history world.

Through a DNA test you will be able to learn the ethnic makeup and migrations of your ancestors and discover new "cousins". DNA test results can help your family history efforts by confirming things you already know as well as connecting you with others. Many people are able to break through the all too common brick walls with the help of a second- or third-cousin whom they have never met.

Everyone's DNA is unique and no two people will have your same genetics unless they are identical twins. Although we can say with some degree of certainty that we have some DNA from each of our four grandparents and possibly from our great grandparents the further back you go in your pedigree the less likely it is that you have inherited DNA from anyone further back.

As with traditional genealogical research, DNA testing can provide surprises so be prepared for the "skeleton in the cupboard". You could easily uncover family secrets as you match with a cousin or a relative that you previously had no contact with or didn't know existed. In some cases, people discover that their parents are not their biological parents but don't let that put you off tasking a test. If you want the small print and the reasoning behind using DNA for genealogy then go to the internet and read the Genetic Genealogy Standards originally established in 2015.

However, DNA testing will not provide you with an instant family tree. You cannot take a DNA test to discover who you are and where you come from. The value of any test is in the comparison process, so it's important to test with a company that has a good matching database set. Most of these are improving all the time as more and more people avail themselves of the tests.

To be most effective you need to use DNA in combination with traditional genealogical records in order to form conclusions about relationships.

The choice of test you take is dependent on the questions and challenge that you want to answer. A DNA test is certainly well worth the cost and the value of the test will grow as more people join the databases and you get more matches.

There are three different types of test – autosomal DNA (aDNA), Y-chromosome DNA (yDNA) and mitochondrial DNA (mtDNA) – all of which have specific applications. Sometimes a combination of different tests will be required to solve a particular problem. For this you will need to consult the companies offering the tests to see which suits you best. Remember DNA is not the answer on its own but another tool to help overcome a challenge.

Briefly DNA tests are as follows: The Y-chromosome is passed from father to son via only the direct male line and therefore is useful for surname studies. Females can't take the test but a close male relative can as a substitute. We all have mitochondrial DNA and so anyone can take this test because this type of DNA is passed from mother to child following the direct female line. Autosomal chromosomes from our parents, half from our father and half from our mother. However, we don't pass this on to our children in equal amounts.

 Make sure the DNA test you are considering will help you with your research challenge. Be aware of the different types of test that are available. Always use the results of a DNA test to complement your own research. Don't use DNA results in isolation.

The best and most economical way to approach DNA testing is to identify one or more individuals in the oldest living generation in your family. If that person is a male then begin with a YDNA test. But in addition, you should also undertake an autosomal DNA test. If that is female begin with the autosomal DNA.

It is not vital initially to have a mtDNA test even though it is a test that can be used by both men and women. In the ideal world you may need to have all three but that is expensive. However, if you have a difficult research challenge on your direct maternal line, or even if you are meticulous in your research you can of course undertake mtDNA testing. It shouldn't be considered high on the priority list as the results aren't always genealogically beneficial. But there may be a hidden gem in that mtDNA test. If you decide to do it, order a Full Sequence mtDNA test.

When you receive your family history DNA test results you will have a list of

DNA matches to contact. Receiving your results and finding out your ethnicity is only the start. When you receive your DNA matches from your testing company you will have a list of potential DNA cousins who may hold valuable information to help you expand your family tree.

So how can you benefit from these DNA matches? Before you contact your matches it's worth making a plan so that you can maximise your chances of a helpful response.

Before contacting a match ensure that your online family tree is up-to-date, particularly if you and your potential DNA matches share one or more common surnames. It is helpful to try and establish which ancestors you might have in common as this will help you should you receive a positive response to your message. If the person you match with has an online family tree that is in the public domain do a search of this too otherwise you will need to be invited in to view the tree after contact is made.

One important aspect to remember is that any matched relationship specified as a result of the DNA test can only be an approximation. Your own research with the help of your DNA match can confirm how the two of you are related. Before contacting your matches be sure to make use of the DNA tools offered by the company with whom you took your test. Different companies may show different results. Some will be more comprehensive than others but all have the potential to resolve research challenges.

When first contacting a DNA match your aim should be to open channels of communication. You can maximise your chances of a reply by including information about the company you tested with because some people test with more than one company, the type of DNA test you took, your username if this is shown on the match site and a link to your online tree and/or surnames list and regions of interest.

GENEALOGICAL PROOF STANDARD – THE GENEALOGY GPS.

Have you demolished your brick wall or overcome your research challenge?

The GPS of family history requires five steps:

Reasonably exhaustive research has been conducted.
Each statement of fact has a complete and accurate source citation.
The evidence is reliable and has been skilfully correlated and interpreted.
Any contradictory evidence has been resolved.
The conclusion has been soundly reasoned and coherently written.

Following the GPS is fundamental to a good proven family tree and authenticates your research. If you intend to publish your findings then it is often a pre-requirement in doing so.

Using the Genealogical Proof Standard from the start will save you a lot of time and effort revisiting former research and examining what you researched before should you have a question about whether your conclusions are correct. It is also useful to have GPS in place if you come across new information that may possibly alter the research you've already done.

Don't let GPS become daunting. Many family historians reach brick walls or challenges because they did not employ it at day one. GPS should give you confidence about the direction your research is taking.

GPS is a methodology that all researchers can use and enhances what has been discussed throughout this book. It is sound advice and if you follow the guidelines, you will end up with quality research, and usually break through those brick walls. Researching family history can become complicated and complex. In your search to find the elusive ancestor, you're likely to come across dozens of records, countless websites and a host of books each offering you a piece of the puzzle. With so much information available, incorporating the GPS into your research allows you to justify your work and feel secure in your conclusions.

Genealogical proof - Analyse and Correctly Interpret the Evidence

You will doubtless be collecting a vast amount of evidence of a family's existence so how you review, look at, sort and analyse the information will determine what you learn about your relative.

Prime sources are more likely to be correct and are primarily the preferred type of sources for genealogy research. Primary information is any information that was reported or recorded at the time, or shortly thereafter.

Secondary sources are not original sources but act as a substitute when originals (prime) sources are not available and is evidence that has been compiled from other sources or that is written after an event occurred by someone who was not present when the event happened.

Resolve Any Contradictory Evidence

"GPS is all about collating information. It is using evidence from various sources to form a conclusion that will stand alone. This step can be frequently overlooked. Every one of us will have found mismatching evidence at some point in our research and possibly discount the information because it did not ally with your gut feeling.

Experienced researchers should understand and expect contradictory evidence. Through your analytical skills you would apply logical reasoning to provide answers for each discrepancy.

Analysing and evaluating evidence is a process that should be continually addressed. The ideal should start at day one of your research as soon as you find a document to see if it is relevant to your family or the individual you are researching. You should be evaluating by carrying out a preliminary evaluation of the reliability of the source, and then by a comparison of information in the document with other information you have about the family to see if it corroborates or contradicts.

Handling contradictory evidence:

By this point you will be continually asking questions either in your mind or by talking to someone. As you come across conflicting information or evidence that you are unsure how to handle, become objective and consider the following questions:

When, why and where was the record created?
Is any relevant information missing or incomplete within the record?
How was the information recorded?
Who created the record?
How reliable is the information in the record (based on primary or secondary sources)?

Become an Expert in Your Area of Records.

Look at the evidence from different angles. Compiling evidence is one thing; making sense of it is another. Look at it from all different angles, in different combinations, in order to find patterns that weren't obvious at first. This is where another pair of eyes is important.

 Only when you have proved beyond reasonable doubt that your research is correct can you be confident that you have traced your correct family tree.

WHAT IF I CANNOT DEMOLISH THE BRICK WALL?

At the risk of repeating myself

Re-examine everything
Search all available sources
Look for additional name variations
Work collateral lines.

Breaking down brick walls can take time, patience and persistence.

It can take years of careful research and sifting to find the facts that you need and you will need to be thorough and careful as you go through each step.

The records you need might not yet be online, so you need to be prepared to patiently find and research original records hands-on.

If you do this consistently you will overcome most of your genealogy brick walls.

Remember - your ancestors definitely left records!

Although there does not appear to be a solution to your challenge now there may well be at some point in the future, so revisit and review. New or different records, indexes etc. are becoming available all the time.

CHALLENGE CASEBOOK

The following are some examples, with possible solutions, of situations which may occur when carrying out research into your family history. I hope that you will find the strategies for solutions of some help, but in any case, they will give you an idea of how to apply the practical aspects of breaking down a research challenge. These examples are all based on real live cases.

RAILWAY WORKER

George Harris was a locomotive driver living in West Ham from about 1900 to 1918. During this time, he spent about 3 years in Peru as a locomotive driver. I cannot find out when he was abroad, who he worked for and other details of his career.

Possible solution:

His service record in this country should be researched first. He more than likely worked for the Great Eastern or perhaps the London, Tilbury and Southend Railway. Both of these ran out of West Ham. Look first at Staff Histories of locomotive drivers working for the Great Eastern held at the National Archives. They are organised by staff number and as this is not known, a thorough search may be necessary. If found, there should be an indication when he went to Peru. He may have left the company or been given a leave of absence. Prior to being a driver, he would have been both an engine cleaner and fireman so he has had quite a long career on the railway. Records of those classes of worker should also be searched. There are no similar surviving records for the London Tilbury and Southend Railway.

English railway workers were in demand by foreign railway companies (the English built and ran many railways around the world). From 1907, significant railway development took place in Peru under the auspices of The Peruvian Corporation which controlled most of the railway companies in the country. The Peruvian Corporation recruited workers from its main office in London. Start with the working files of the Corporation 1849-1959 archived at University College, London and include records of most of the Peru Railway Companies.

SHIPS COOK

In the 1901 census Peter Robert Johnson is a ships' cook on board HM Yacht Ophir which was chartered by the government as a Royal Yacht and was travelling to Australia with HRH Prince George and other members of the Royal Family. Cannot find a Royal Navy record for Peter so which branch of the Royal Navy would he belong to? As he cannot be found in 1891 I assume he was on another ship.

Ophir was in fact a civilian ship owned by the Orient Line and would have received the designation H M Yacht only for the duration of the voyage to Australia. As such all the crew members would have been from the Merchant Navy employed directly by the Orient Line rather than from the Royal Navy (although some Royal Navy personnel may have been on board).

Ophir was built in 1891 in Glasgow and sailed between England and Australia which is why I suspect it was chartered. There were only a couple of times within the history of Royal Yachts where merchant vessels were used. In this instance it was because of a Navy supply commitment to the South African War.

To find his records look at surviving records of the Merchant Navy, he should have a seaman's ticket. However, certificates of competency for cooks were not introduced until 1906 so you may not find any record of the time period of his service (unless he served through World War One) is when many records were destroyed. Find his details on the crew lists and agreements, but for Ophir in 1901 these are likely to be in Newfoundland which you can apply for online if you know the official number of a ship. The first avenue is the National Maritime Museum at Greenwich which houses records, including staff records, for P & O into which the Orient Line was merged.

AT A BARNARDO RUN SCHOOL BUT NOT AN ORPHAN?

On the 1911 census John Wilson was resident at the Watts Naval School at Elmham in Norfolk. Trying to find records for 1910-1920 but have been unsuccessful. It appears the school was maintained by Barnardo. How can we access the records? John was not an orphan so I am not sure how he got there.

Possible solution:

Watts Naval School was originally a County private school established to provide education for "sons of farmers and artisans". That school closed in 1895 and was re-established by a Mr E H Watts, a London ship owner, who acquired the property at auction in 1901. Following his death, the school became part of the Barnardo organisation and was used to train boys for the Royal Navy opening in March 1903. It accommodated 300 pupils and provided two years of general education then when reaching the age of 14yrs they received two years of naval training. After this the boys went on to complete their training on HMS Ganges, a Royal Navy training establishment in Suffolk. The training school admission criteria was that pupils were orphan or destitute, between 11 and 14 yrs, but evidence suggests that in the early years it still took "sons of farmers and artisans" who specifically sought a navy career which may explain how John became a pupil.

Records of the school are in various locations. The admission registers up to 1932 and various editions of Jack Tar, the school magazine are at Norfolk County Record Office but administration records and minutes may form part of the Barnardo archive at Liverpool University Library Special Collections and Archives.

TRACING A BIRTH CERTIFICATE OF A BRITISH CITIZEN BORN ABROAD

How can I trace the birth certificate of Frederick Maddocks who was born 22 May 1866 in Lugano, Italy and returned to this country with his parents when he was about 4yrs old. He married twice and have his marriage details which show his father as William on one and as William John Maddocks on the other, both record his occupation as gentleman. Cannot find him in later census returns either.

Possible solution:

I think the geography is slightly misinterpreted. Whilst it is commonly thought that Lugano is in Italy, the city itself is in the Ticino Canton of Switzerland and certainly was in 1866. The Swiss were generally good at keeping vital records from the 17th century onwards but their registration systems are maintained at Canton level. Contact Ticino Canton Archives in Switzerland. They may be able to help with tracing the birth if it was Swiss registered.

However, as he appears to have been born of British parentage you may find his birth was registered with the British Consul in Switzerland. It is worth looking at the births abroad indexes. If found the certificate can be obtained online from the GRO

You may also have to undertake a blanket search of all post 1871 census returns. If Frederick returned as a youngster he may have assumed he was born in England and thus appears with an English birthplace. I would not think the name Frederick Maddocks is that common so undertake eliminating research on any found who were born around 1866. You should also try and locate any of Frederick's siblings as it is sometimes by side-tracking that vital clues are found.

COALMINER'S STINT IN AMERICA

Robert Welbeck Addis, an English coal miner from Northumberland, went to Pennsylvania in the 1860s and returned to England in 1877 having had two sons born there in 1872 and 1877. Robert's brother, William, also a miner, emigrated about the same time. Why did they go and why did Robert return to England? Can we locate copies of his children's birth certificates?

Possible solution:

Civil registration of births in parts of Pennsylvania began in 1870 but was not common until c1906 so you may not locate birth certificates for the two sons. You should also look at the US Social Security Index for details of William as he stayed in the USA.

Unless you have a record indicating the coal mine where Robert and his brother worked in this country you may not be able to find conclusive proof why he went to America. In Pennsylvania around this time the coal mining industry was at strength with prominent British mine owners also having American interests. Most of the manual mining jobs in Pennsylvania were carried out by a British labour force taken there by the owners. The Durham Mining Museum may have more background information.

By the mid to late 1870s there was a significant decline in Pennsylvania mining as coal could not compete with the new natural gas fields. This resulted in a general depression forcing many miners to return home. Robert could have been amongst them. The Stanton family who owned mines in Northumberland and Durham were involved with mining in Westmorland County Pennsylvania and suffered pit closures so it is possible that they may have transferred their miners back to the UK. There may have been similar situations where other companies also brought their workforce back home.

Index